Published by Ockley Books Limited

First published February 2018

ISBN 978-1-910906-12-5

Layout & design by Michael Kinlan,
edited by David Hartrick

Extra illustrations by Fred Bosence

Printed & bound by:

Biddles Printing, King's Lynn

OCKLEY BOOKS
.com

PRELUDE

We are sorry to inform you that the Publishing Board has decided that the above work is not something that it feels able to take on at the moment.

Thank you for taking the time to submit your work to us and we sincerely wish you every success in placing your manuscript elsewhere.

Unfortunately we don't believe your book could be a commercial success as a traditional publishing project, the trade market is extremely unforgiving at the moment and your book is pretty niche...

I have now read your book, which is very well written, well paced & a very enjoyable read. I really enjoyed it and congratulate you on writing a very good book. You capture the fun & frustration of being a football fan at a team which means a lot locally, but is never likely to become a top club and win the big prizes.

Much as I enjoyed it I am sorry to say that we are unable to publish it. If we were one of the big sports book publishers I would take a gamble on it, but as a small publisher each book we publish must fund itself and hopefully, contribute to the growth of the business and generate some profit.

Our refusal is not based on the writing but on the likely market for the book, which we feel is too small to cover our costs and make a modest profit.

I am really sorry to have to say No but would encourage

you to try other publishers or at least to self publish and keep writing. If it was about Liverpool, who get several mentions, or one of the other big Premier League clubs it would have a bigger market, but would probably not have the same charm and light touch.

Also I would respectfully suggest you move so you are not constantly supplying your neighbour with things, although I agree with your point about the cost of diesel when you only want something low cost or in small quantity. However your relationship with him is part of the charm of the book. Also your point about us men talking about football rather than dealing with our emotions is well made.

You are definitely a talented writer and I hope you will keep writing.

Many thanks for your Plymouth Argyle book submission. Unfortunately a fans view/diary of a team can be difficult to sell. It can sometimes work when there is a special reason and the club is big enough, however I think with Plymouth Argyle the sales potential is too limited for ourselves. I'm therefore going to turn down your offer.

Candidly, based on the size of the market and likely sales (e.g. in the hundreds), self-publishing would probably be your best way to maximize returns. I am not sure that our company could bring enough value-add to the party to make the book more of a success than you could manage. I wish you all the best with the project.

Thanks for submission and book, which I received this morning.

It's not for us I'm afraid. It's a bit too short and a bit too personal.

You may wonder why I'm coming back to you so quickly. The reason is you happened to hit upon a Plymouth Argyle supporter who first went to Home Park in the mid-fifties. We lost 6-1 in the cup at home to Newcastle. I was lifted over the heads of the crowd and sat behind the goal at the Devonport Road End. I remember Wilf Carter missing a sitter and being totally bemused by the Newcastle left winger Bobby Mitchell.

So my advice would be to publish it yourself and market it through the usual Argyle outlets. You'll probably make more money that way. But first you need to correct one error I spotted...

BARNET AWAY GRAND COMPETITION

As pointed out by the commissioning editor above, there is one error concerning a footballing fact (that we know about - there may be more). I did not make this mistake intentionally.

The first 100 people to correctly point out the mistake that I have made will receive a very special, limited edition, numbered book mark, commissioned by the author, to celebrate two great seasons of being an Argyle fan.

Please email your answer to barnetaway@barnetaway.com.

TO ALEX. YOU NEVER HIT THE BIG TIME,
BUT IN YOUR MIND YOU DID.

BY JOSH WIDDICOMBE

I should have been an Exeter fan. They were the first team I went to see when I was seven (a 1-0 win, of which my main memory is my surprise that there was no commentary within the stadium), they were my nearest league team as a child and they had a nice kit. But instead I decided to chase the glory and became a Plymouth Argyle fan. I have no regrets, despite choosing the Real Madrid of Devon. I still have the moral high ground in most conversations with football fans, the kind of people who opt to support Arsenal or Liverpool — or even Real Madrid — because their uncle happened to have trials for them in the 1970s. "What a pathetic reason to support a football team," I'll think to myself, as if there is such a thing as a good one. I certainly don't have any real reason at all to support Plymouth: I was born in London, I went to school near Exeter, my friends supported Man U, my dad followed Liverpool and my mum owns a Tottenham scarf (reason unconfirmed).

The decision to support Argyle has delivered me more than 25 years of bad football, five relegations, a half-finished stadium, a chip on my shoulder about Burnley, and a season watching an ageing Bruce Grobbelaar keep goal even though he couldn't train in the week as he was appearing in court. But in a way this is a good thing, my moral ground has become higher and higher as Plymouth have sunk lower and lower through the years. I dread the day that we make it into the Premier League and suddenly I'm just another fan watching my team play at 8pm on a Monday night on Sky Sports. My God those Bournemouth fans must miss the lower leagues.

The reason I like football is how well balanced it is. I went to watch a basketball game when I was in New York a year or two ago; what a dreary sport that is. Too many points — where are the huge moments of excitement? The reason that football is the greatest sport ever invented (and, for the record, it definitely is) is that goals are rare. You will probably see one if you go to a match (occasionally for your team) but they are unlikely enough that when it happens it is a great moment; it was worth the other 89 minutes of frustration. Well, factor that over 25 years and that is what supporting Plymouth is like — maybe three or four truly great moments, made all the sweeter because of what came between.

I probably wouldn't have stuck around so loyally for those moments if it hadn't been that my dad and my brother were going through the same thing. Maybe I would have become more interested in my dad's Premier League team Liverpool as a child or, when I moved to London, maybe I would have started going to watch Arsenal as they were my local team (and successful!), but that is now not what having a team is about for us. It is a shared experience between three people who live in different parts of the country. Even in the 34 years of my life, the idea of shared experiences has become less and less a part of people's lives. People can consume TV programmes or films whenever and wherever they want, usually on their own while wearing headphones. I can't remember the last time I had a conversation with someone about something we both watched the night before, except for sport. For my family, Argyle has become our way of making sure we have a shared identity and experience; every time they play we are bound together, even if it is only dad at the match and me checking it on the Sky Sports app.

I will always be pleased to be a Plymouth fan. It is not that I identify with the city, or the history of the club (I am always doubtful of fans who claim their club is special in some way or has a different character to others, they are like people who think their baby is infinitely more interesting than everyone else's) and it is not because they have given me the greatest moments of my life. For me there is far more to life than how my team is doing, I'm afraid. I know that may not make me sound like the heroic loyalist that a lot of fans paint themselves to be, but I really am over a defeat by about 6pm on the Saturday. Simply, I like being a Plymouth fan because it is something that brings my family together, as this book demonstrates, and it feels right that this is being told through the story of a disappointing away defeat to a rubbish team. That's Argyle.

BARNET AWAY

TOM WIDDICOMBE

PART ONE

GREAT ESCAPES, SUPER SIXES & BARNET AWAY

My friend Alex came in from down at the farm. He'd had a traumatic night. Over the last 24 hours one of his girlfriend Sam's horses had gone from being perfectly OK to being so ill that he had called the vet at three in the morning to come over and end its life.

The dead horse was on the floor of the stable and Alex needed to borrow the tractor to pull the body out to be picked up by the digger. The plan was to get the horse buried before Sam got back later that morning to avoid further upset. Now, I've seen quite a few dead horses in my life, and I've got used to it a bit, but this was the first time anything like this had happened to Alex. He was pretty shaken up and I could see that he was close to tears. I'm not great at sympathy and I kind of just stood there trying not to make things any worse. Then out of nowhere, Alex said, "How did you get on with your Super 6 this week?"

That was it. We then had a long conversation about football. Alex is good at talking about football, and one of his major theories is that a lot of blokes, and no doubt some women, use football as a convenient way of avoiding discussing the more difficult issues of life. That morning I stood there in our kitchen with Alex talking football, all of the time totally aware that the conversation we were having was allowing us to be together without me or him having to deal with all the emotion of the last 24 hours.

Football; life's great escape.

27TH FEBRUARY 2016, NOTTS COUNTY (H)

I've been to quite a few Argyle games this season. This particular Saturday it's Notts County at Home Park. I like to get to the ground early to give myself plenty of time to go through my routines:

1. Pick up on the atmosphere outside the stadium;

2. Check to see if there are any new fanzines;

3. If I'm really early, a little browse around the club shop is called for, now unbelievably named 'The Argyle Retail Outlet';

4. Into the ground to buy a cup of tea and watch the players doing their warm-ups.

I like being on my own at the match. I enjoy being with my own thoughts. Like most fans, I think I know quite a bit about the game. In reality, I probably don't, but when did that ever stop us dreaming? I am standing by the barrier drinking my tea and I've made sure I'm a good couple of yards away from anyone so there is no danger of being engaged in conversation. But unbelievably, and perhaps inevitably, it happens. This young girl comes and stands right by me and says, "What do you think the score will be today?" It is only an opening line to start a conversation, but as you now know, I do the Super 6.

I know predicting scores is a complete shot in the dark. Guessing the score in public like this? Well, it's just something I would never do. But then again she's a young fan, maybe 15 years old, and just trying to be friendly. So I give it a bit of thought and go for the old favourite: 2-1 to us. That sounds pretty feasible. I ask her if she always comes to football on her own and she tells me she normally comes with her dad but he is working. She tells me she is a Chelsea supporter and I tell her I hate them. I probably shouldn't but it's a natural reaction. She is worried about sitting in a different seat to the one she has a ticket for. I tell her not to worry and that I do it all the time. At half time I offer to buy her a hot chocolate but she says no. In the end Argyle play really well and we win the game 1-0. That'll do.

Only five years ago Plymouth Argyle were in real trouble. The club was docked 10 points when it went into administration. A couple of weeks later, an inevitable relegation to League Two followed. The following two seasons, Argyle were seriously in danger of dropping out of the League — actually spending weeks and weeks at the bottom of the table — but thankfully they eventually finished in 21st position for two years running. Things have really picked up recently. Last season (2014/15) we made the play-offs and this year we were top of the League at Christmas.

On Boxing Day, we played Yeovil at home and won 1-0. It was a difficult game and I came away worrying whether our position at the top of the League was giving a false impression of how good we actually were. I admit that my view is slightly coloured by the experiences of the last 20 or so years following Argyle. Supporting a club through so many ups and downs, living through so many cliffhangers, so many 'nearly' moments — it all takes its toll. It is also no easier emotionally to be top than bottom. History and experience tends to dissolve any belief that you have at either end, but in those times when things are going well the slightest knock-back turns into the beginning of the end. Following a team like Argyle is not an easy ride, it's a full-on lesson in the duality of life. I've lost count of the number of times I've walked away from Home Park telling myself not to worry, it's only football.

If you study our results since Boxing Day, although it feels like we are stuttering a bit the fact is we are not doing too badly. We have won five, drawn four and lost three. Eighteen points from 10 games doesn't sound terrible does it? But the reality is we have also dropped 12 points, lost our top spot, and are now in big danger of facing the much-dreaded play-offs. I really don't want to go through another play-off scenario, but right now it is beginning to look like a real possibility.

The Notts County game was absolutely crucial. I know that, in the situation we're in, all games are crucial, but if you start losing at home to teams in the bottom half of the table? Well, that really does knock the wind out of your sails. It was great to get the result, we only won by the odd goal but the real bonus for me was that we played well. I came away from the game really fired up and my faith restored. Still a little voice nagged in the back of my mind somewhere that it's the hope that kills you, but three points just about drowned it out. Until the next game of course.

Leaving Home Park after the match is never dull. I always stay at least until the final whistle, and sometimes hang about to acknowledge the players' efforts when they come over to thank the fans. I park on the other side of Central Park and I enjoy the walk back to the car. If we've won, I bathe in the euphoria of supporting a winning team. If we've lost, I go into a more philosophical mood and ponder the futility of being a football supporter.

About two-thirds of the way across the park, the path leads through some large allotments and I always study the progress of the crops. Without fail, they are ahead of mine: up here on the moor we are 1,000 feet higher, and 25 miles further east – our crops are always several weeks behind. I imagine what it would be like to live in a city and have an allotment, and then I remember back 30-odd years ago, to the short time we lived in Bristol and we had an allotment quite near to Ashton Gate.

Before I reach the car, a text comes through from my son Josh: 'Barnet on Tuesday?'

Oh my God, I'm so tempted. 'I'll have to see how things are nearer the time,' I text back.

On the drive home, my joy soon turns to extreme annoyance. I turn the radio on to enjoy the football scores and it turns out they are broadcasting a rugby commentary. How on earth can that happen? Whoever took that decision? I mean... For goodness' sake... Every week thousands and thousands of fans around the country get into their cars at five o'clock on a Saturday and turn the radio on to listen to the scores coming in — was it a good result or a *really* good result? Do any of those fans care two hoots about a game of rugby? Not very many, I bet. I am fuming.

I turn the radio off and my thoughts drift back to the days when I was young and free. Truth is, those days only exist in my mind. Obvious statement I know, unless of course you believe in some obscure parallel universe-type of situation that even now I am struggling to get my head around. But when I think about it there was actually a time, when I left school, when I did feel young and free. I can tell you exactly how long it lasted too. I was 17 when I decided enough was enough as far as learning stuff I wasn't interested in was concerned. I took the decision to be free, but then I lost my nerve and jumped back in to learn some more. I went to college for a second try. Alas no, I was not cut out for it, and I was soon back out on the road again. My young and free years lasted from the age of 19 to the age of 23. At that point, my parental responsibilities kicked in, and my wild life came to an abrupt end.

I never once, in the whole of those four years, thought about football — that I can say with absolute certainty. Ah no, now I come to think about it, I am in a team photo taken at Black Rock Sands in North Wales in 1971. It's coming back to me now, we played a 6-a-side game on the beach and someone recorded the event for posterity on a black-and-white film. I have no idea which team won, and I can't remember any details about the game. It was one of those late 1960s moments that had drifted on a couple of years into the early 1970s and is now filed under the heading: *If you remember that game then you weren't actually playing in it.*

If anyone had studied my early playing career they would surely have realised I was not destined for great things. I made a few appearances for Padbury United in the North Bucks and District League. Only once was I actually selected to play for the team, all my other appearances came as a reserve who got to play due to other players failing to turn up.

In 1963 I answered an advert in the local paper for under-15 teams to play in a new Aylesbury and District League. We asked a farmer if we could make a pitch on one of his flat fields just outside the village. Five teams entered the League, which was then completely dominated by a team called Hazels, from Aylesbury. Our worst result was against them away. We lost 16-0. The following year, Padbury United was formed and they played on our pitch. The under-15 team was discontinued. I got the job of washing the team's bright yellow shirts for £5 per week.

Padbury United's headquarters were at the Blackbird pub in the middle of the village. The team list for the next match was always pinned up on the noticeboard outside the pub at around six o'clock on Wednesday. My brother Phil and I used to walk down to the pub during the evening to see if we had been selected to play. Phil was always up there on the list. He was a shoo-in at no.11; a tricky little left-winger who could guarantee to get in a few good crosses in every match. I was sometimes up on the board — as the reserve. That's apart from the one time which I mentioned earlier. That week I was an automatic choice at no.9. How this unlikely event came about was all down to my performance the previous week. I was the reserve and I ended up playing at centre-forward. I can't imagine how it happened. The selected striker didn't turn up, but I'd have thought they'd have chosen to play me in a less important position. But, anyway, they didn't and that's where I played. Not once but twice the ball got crossed from the wing and both times I was in the perfect spot to head it into the back of the net. Unbelievable I know, but true. And we won the game.

The next Wednesday, full of trepidation, I walked down to look at the noticeboard. Surely now I would be given my chance. I needn't have worried. There it was, my name, right there in at no.9. Saturday came but alas the game didn't go so well. Not one cross anywhere near me. In fact, I might as well not have been on the pitch. I remember my frustration getting the better of me in that game too. I remember actually shouting the words: "How can I score if you don't give me the ball?"

Such words of wisdom. I learnt a lot about football that day.

***

I've just Googled Padbury United. There is a local newspaper article up there from 2011, headlined "Dream becomes a nightmare as Padbury FC folds".

It seems the club, still nicknamed the Blackbirds, was bankrolled by local businessman Dr Phil Smith, who had ambitions to turn it into the biggest club in the area after the MK Dons. In 2010 Padbury were Division Two champions in the South Midlands League. The article also correctly states that the club was founded in 1964, but unfortunately there was no mention of either of my goals.

It turns out that in 2011, the club was involved in a ground share with Buckingham Town who then lost their ground. Padbury were unable to find another home in time for the beginning of the season. The manager and eight of the players left to join another local club called Ampthill United.

The same article gives details of a new club being formed that will play on Padbury playing fields in the North Bucks League. The club is to be called The Real Padbury United, a catchy team name if ever there was one. In the article, a founding member explains that the new club is for the people of Padbury, and that most of those playing for the other Padbury United came from Milton Keynes anyway. There is a team photo taken a couple of years later showing the new club playing in the familiar yellow shirts again.

Twenty-four hours after our victory over Notts County and I am still pondering on the possibility of Barnet away. I definitely want to go but I have some big responsibilities here at home that are weighing really heavily on me. I have my business to run, and my granddaughter to look after, plus a lot of jobs that I normally do around the place to keep the show on the road. I've checked the trains and, unbelievably, Exeter to London takes just over two hours. I can do the whole trip in under 24 hours, which is not always the case living where we do. I've even checked the ticket prices and they're not too bad either — £84 for a return.

I am worried about getting from Paddington to Barnet. I know if you are a regular user of The Tube you are probably thinking: "worried about what?". But you see, some years ago, in fact the last time I travelled to London by train, I had to get from Paddington to the Eurotunnel terminus, and I screwed up on The Tube and missed my train. The online guides are telling me it is 40 minutes from Paddington to Canons Park, and then a five-minute walk to the ground. That sounds all too similar to the missed-train fiasco of the Eurotunnel trip.

It doesn't take much to turn 40 minutes into an hour, or even quite a bit more. One or two elementary mistakes — like messing up on the ticket machines or taking the odd wrong turn — and suddenly you're in a nightmare. But one big thing has swung in my favour: my dear and beautiful wife has given me the green light. She is happy for me to go and confident that she can manage to hold the fort while I am away. This trip is starting to look like a real possibility.

I've worked out all the train times and The Tube route to the ground. I have this military operation in hand and there will be no Eurotunnel nightmare repeat. All I need to do now is to press the 'buy' button. So I do. That's it, I've bought the train tickets and in two days' time I will be on my way to Barnet to watch Plymouth Argyle, hopefully, take another big step towards League One. Barnet are 15th in the League but they are far from being a pushover. They have 40 points from 33 games and have recently beaten Portsmouth and Bristol Rovers, and drawn with Accrington — all teams strongly challenging for promotion with us.

Barnet are managed by Martin Allen. That sounds a familiar name to me. It sounds like a West Ham player, or at least from that kind of area anyway. So I look him up. Yep, he played for QPR, West Ham, Portsmouth and, right at the end of his career, he played five games for Southend. But things start to get really interesting when you look at his managerial career. In 12 years of management he has had 10 managerial contracts, including four spells as manager of Barnet. The current one is by far his longest and most successful period at the club. Last season he took them up from the Conference as champions.

But it is his previous job as manager of Gillingham that interests me. He joined them in July 2012 and won the League Two championship, and he was also named League Two Manager of the Season. Then, the following season he was sacked after winning just two of his first 11 games. That sounds a bit harsh to me. I know that sometimes a manager loses his way and a change can make a dramatic difference, but to go from Manager of the Year to being sacked 11 games into the season? Really? That's either ridiculously harsh or there was more to it.

So, how much benefit did Gillingham get from changing their manager at that point in the season? Allen was replaced by Peter Taylor. In the remaining 35 games of the season, he took them up to 17th with a total for the season of 53 points. The following season he was sacked or, as it says on Wikipedia, 'relieved of his duties' in December. In this case, I would say the evidence that the change of manager was beneficial is not conclusive either way.

But, and this is a big 'but', after Allen was 'relieved of his duties' by Gillingham he joined Barnet, and the following season they won the Conference. That makes two titles in three years. You have to start to think, or from a Plymouth perspective right now worry, that maybe he has a bit of an idea how football works.

It's Sunday evening and I am in the shed sorting out a few tools so that things won't be too chaotic when I return from the match on Wednesday. There is a knock on the door and Alex appears.

"Hi Tom. I was wondering if you have any three-inch nails you could spare?"

"Sure Alex. What are they for? What's the job?"

"I'm just cladding a shed. Any nails will do really."

"Oh right," I reply, "but if you're using tanalised timber, you'll need galvanised nails."

"Really, why?"

"Well, the tantalising will rot the nails. You definitely have to use galvanised."

"Oh shit," says Alex, followed by a small pause as things sink in.

"I've just done three-quarters of the job and I had no idea about that."

"Ah well," I say, "hopefully we'll be long gone before that cladding all falls off the wall anyway."

And then, completely unprompted by me but enforced by the weight of the error in the air, Alex starts to talk about football. The great escape again.

Alex is a Liverpool supporter. He's the bloke who got me into doing Super 6. We made a League but only he and I are in it. And because he started at the beginning of the season and I missed a few games, he is ahead of me at the moment. I started to say that it was a shame the Super 6 app didn't average out your score per game to make it easier to see who is best. And then we looked at the leaderboard. Alex is 915,357th and I am 980,752nd. I have 106 points. I checked how many weeks I've entered this season — it's 11, so my average is 9.63. So I go to the Global Top Fifteen. The guy in first place has 337 points. We are in week 35, so assuming he has entered every week, which he surely has, his average is 9.62.

OK, so the point isn't about my average being the same as his, it's more about how I really would have expected the leading averages to be way higher than they are. If you are not familiar with how Super 6 works, there are six games and you have to predict the scores of all of them. You get five points for a correct score and two points if you get the result correct but the score wrong. So maximum points would be 30 all in per matchday.

You pretty soon realise that getting correct scores is not easy at all, so getting six correct scores is pretty much impossible. Getting correct results is more doable. When you fill in your entry, Skybet offers you odds on your six results being correct. These odds vary depending on how near your predictions are to theirs (obviously). I normally get offered around the region of 200/1. One time my predictions were wildly out and I was offered huge odds of around 2,000/1, which I took. And, not surprisingly, at five o'clock on the Saturday afternoon Sky took my money. I checked with my friend John, who is a mathematician, what the odds are on getting six correct results alone — win, lose, or draw — by chance. The odds are 729/1.

Anyway, the way I am thinking is this: if you are pretty knowledgeable about the Premier League you should be able to predict three or four results most weeks, which is six or eight points, and now and again you are going to predict a correct score which would make that total up to nine or 11 points, so averaging just under ten doesn't seem that difficult. In theory anyway. I'd better just say, sometimes they do chuck in the odd Championship game which is a bit more tricky, and sometimes they use Cup games, which is chaotic to say the least. But generally speaking, I'd say three or four results is a realistic target. Time will tell I guess. Maybe right now I'm fluking it and I have a points-drought just up ahead. We'll see.

Alex takes a bunch of three-inch galvanised nails and leaves. I carry on sorting tools. I begin to think about his theory that blokes talk about football to avoid the possibility of talking about any other awkward subject in life. It dawns on me that not only is it a pretty sound theory, it is also most definitely a lifestyle technique Alex employs, possibly as some kind of earthing mechanism.

I begin to wonder if he is experiencing some kind of mental state that he's using football conversation to control. You know, a bit like when things get tense and you make a joke, or when you make small talk about a familiar subject to try to take your mind off a desperate situation. Alex is a master of the football conversation. He has clearly been talking about it for many years. There is no end to the depth that the conversations can go to, but they never stray very far away from the core subject of football itself.

And then I realise that I do the very same thing myself. I am in a texting group with my two sons, Henry and Josh, and my wife Sarah. The group is called 'Pure Argyle Chat'. We communicate a lot through this group, and I would conservatively say the more than 95 per cent of our conversation is about football. I rarely have conversations with my sons outside of this group, and when I do, we are usually at a match, so those conversations are mostly about football anyway. The circle is complete, if you like.

Of course, the situation with Sarah is very different. Only the other day I had a real-life conversation with her that wasn't about football. Also it was a conversation in which I truly showed my emotional side. I was trying to establish if she had any plans for Saturday afternoon, clearing the ground to ask if it was OK for me to make my customary visit to Home Park. She always acts as though she doesn't know the question is coming — which is really annoying — but she said that she was happy for me to go anyway. I punched the air and shouted "Come On You Greens!", and then I realised I was revealing far too much of myself, and I quickly regained a semblance of control.

***

It's Monday morning, the day before the game. I have to go and look at some tools in Totnes, so I decide to take my train ticket printout to the station and get my tickets. Last time — the day of *that* Eurotunnel fiasco — I got to Exeter station and couldn't get the automatic ticket machine to work. A queue was building up behind me and I was really feeling the pressure. Thank God the young lady behind me took pity on me, or more likely thought "for God's sake, you silly old fool, let me do it for you". Anyway, for whatever reason, she kindly helped me get my tickets and I was on my way.

One thing I have noticed as I have got older is that I have got a little better at what they would call in an office 'Forward Performance Strategy' or what I would call, planning ahead. (I really hate office jargon, so if we ever meet up please avoid using it around me, OK?) The perfect example of my earned-in-later-life skill, I quickly worked out that if I pick up the tickets the day before rather than when I arrive at the station to catch my train, that cuts out a huge amount of potential time, and more importantly pressure, that could be caused by being late or not being able to work the machine or whatever pitfall happened to come my way that day.

I easily find the house where the guy has the tools for sale. He has a good collection there and we agree a price that we are both happy with. I load them into the van and set off to the station. I spend a lot of time in Totnes. It is a sweet little town and I feel at home there. I turn into Station Road and a gentleman waves me towards a spacious parking area. It is all very easy. Maybe too easy?

I walk onto the platform and find the ticket machine. I know it might not sound like it, but I am a pretty IT-friendly bloke. I am good with my phone and reasonably good with my computer. Quite often I help other people sort out some of the more basic problems they have with this kind of stuff. But, for some reason, public machines like this one seem to completely freeze me. It's the same with self-service tills in supermarkets, cash machines outside banks, and even parking ticket machines; I just don't like them and they can smell my fear.

I stand in front of the machine and look at it. I read the instructions. I try a few obvious things, and nothing seems to be working. After a few minutes I begin to wonder if it might be possible to get the tickets from an actual human instead. Thank God I'm not doing this tomorrow in Exeter with a train to catch. The station is very quiet, in fact not a soul about. I make a conscious effort to relax and try again. I will not be defeated by this metal box once more. Somehow I realise almost immediately that I've not seen the large touchscreen to the left that allows me to use the machine. Thank

> God this station is empty. I slowly and steadily go through the process step-by-step, and yes, I get my golden tickets. I check that they are correct. They are. I put them safely in my wallet and drive home feeling pretty pleased with my mission so far.

Things have definitely changed a lot since Derek Adams took over as manager of Argyle in June 2015. Reading the details of his management career in Scotland prior to his move to Argyle, I'd say he is quite an impressive addition to the Argyle staff. His stats indicate that he could well be a kind of minor Alex Ferguson figure. One of those cool, one-pointed, and extremely intelligent Scotsmen who, it has to be said, make really good managers.

Apart from a small break, he spent seven years managing Ross County, a small club based in the Scottish Highlands. In that time, he won two promotions and then managed to keep them in the Scottish Premiership for two successive seasons (they are still a Premiership club, now managed by a guy called Jim McIntyre. Maybe we should remember that name?). The highlight of Adams' Ross County management career was undoubtedly the unbeaten run of 40 League games, which included promotion to the Premiership before it was ended by St Johnstone in September 2012.

So how did Plymouth Argyle manage to entice a manager of that calibre to Home Park? I'd say the likelihood is that he sees Argyle as a stepping stone into English football. One can only hope not. In fact, let's hope he is a total dreamer whose childhood ambition is to take a League Two club into the Premier League in England, as well as in Scotland. I don't know a lot about Derek Adams aside from reading his comments in the *Plymouth Herald*, and, perhaps more tellingly, watching his team play football. I'd say the two most impressive things about his team are: firstly, they definitely look like they are really trying for him, and secondly, they do try to play football (most of the time).

I've sat through a lot of Argyle matches in the distant and not-too-distant past, where I have to confess it did look to me like some of the players were just taking the money. I have often left Home Park feeling as if I'd been cheated out of my entrance fee — not a good feeling. But this season that has definitely not been the case. Even in the games we've lost, the classic being our 2-1 defeat by Exeter in November, accepting the defeat was made a little easier by the fact that the players clearly gave their all. That, above all else, in case any footballers ever read this, is what the fans really want from their team.

I just want to say something about that Exeter game, though. Exeter scored both goals early on... actually well into the first half, but it seemed like early on. We just seemed to panic. As soon as Argyle went behind we reverted to route-one football, and, as usual, it didn't really work. It is something of a habit with Argyle, but with this team it is doubly galling because you know that they are capable of playing really good football.

Obviously the game against Exeter comes with huge pressures. It is our massive local derby, and there is a fierce rivalry between the two clubs. There were 14,000 fans at the game, including nearly 1,000 from Exeter. To their credit, the Exeter fans were pretty amazing on that day. Had they been losing, they would have been a bit quieter though, for sure. I have no doubt the Argyle players were feeling the pressure. It was a game that we expected to win. We were having a really good season and theirs wasn't anything special, and suddenly they pitch up at Home Park and actually play really well. The power of local derbies, etc, etc.

But the point I want to make is this: surely it is the responsibility of the manager to say or do something when his team is obviously panicking? Or, and I suppose this is a possibility, Adams actually wants them to play long-ball. I doubt that though, because one thing I have noticed is that the team usually comes out after half time a bit more focussed on playing football, which indicates the nature of the half-time team talk. But in pressure situations, you do see the post-half time focus slip away quite quickly, and surely that is the point where the manager needs to get out there and encourage his players to calm down and just play. Is there anyone left who still believes that randomly kicking the ball up the pitch is a more likely way to win games than by playing football? I know that debate isn't over yet, especially among the fans, but I reckon it should be.

We got a goal back in the 61st minute, leaving loads of time to find an equaliser. Why, oh why, did we play the last half hour as though we were playing in the last two minutes of added time? Still, at least our goalie Luke McCormick didn't run up the other end for every corner and free kick that was lobbed into the area, so I guess that was a bonus.

I get back home from Totnes and unload the tools into the shed. I sort through them, putting all the good stuff that I can sell on one side and the rest out the back to sell to my mate John in Okehampton, who then sells them on at car boot sales. In walks Alex, and this time I'm ready for it. How long will it be before he starts the conversation about football?

"You haven't got any six-by-one tanalised timber lying about have you, Tom?" he asks.

"No mate, I'm pretty sure I haven't," I reply.

"I'm just a couple of lengths short of finishing that job. Never mind, I'll have to go down the builders' merchants."

"That's a nuisance, Alex. Are there any other jobs you can combine in with the journey to make it more worthwhile?" I say. The thing is, living out here I am really aware of the economics of leaving the place to pick up one small item. You end up using a fiver's worth of diesel and, into the bargain, you lose half of your afternoon. I always try to put a load of errands together into one mission, it just feels more productive.

"No, but I don't mind a trip out," Alex replies. "Are you going to be back from London in time to watch the Liverpool match on Wednesday night?"

Ha, so how long was that? Two, maybe three minutes at a stretch? Not that I mind really. I am more than happy to discuss Wednesday's match against Man City.

(What a cruncher that turned out to be, and only three days after Liverpool lost to them in the League Cup Final in a penalty shootout; a terrible penalty shootout at that. Liverpool went one up after the first penalty and then missed the next three, and it was all over. What a dreadful way to end a game, but hey, that's not what this book is all about.)

The thing is that in the 1970s and 1980s there really was only one team, and that was Liverpool at least until Alex Ferguson took over at Manchester United. Then there was still only one team, but it wasn't Liverpool, it was Man U. In those days everything about Liverpool was good: the football, the manager, the club ethos, and the fans. Watching them, for me only ever on the telly, was always a good experience. They were really my introduction to how football should be played, and I became a huge admirer of the club. I still am.

When Brendan Rodgers' reign came to an end and Jürgen Klopp came in, my hopes rose that once again they would be able to hold their own up there with the big boys. Obviously, I had similar hopes when Luis Suarez's genius took them to within a whisker of winning the title a couple of years ago.

The conversation that followed with Alex could neatly be titled: 'Who do you think Kloppy will keep in the squad next season?' My main interest in it was an observation on a couple of the players that Alex definitely thinks will be on their way. Firstly, Daniel Sturridge has to go because he is a prima donna who spends too much time on the injury list, and apparently he's not that good anyway. Secondly, Simon Mignolet has to go too, he's just too unreliable. (Remember these are Alex's ideas, not mine.) The view I put forward was that Kloppy has the squad working really well for him, and, with the knowledge that we have, as distant spectators, it would be impossible to say which are his kind of players and which are not.

Let's use Mignolet as an example here, and in truth there are parallels with how we view all footballers these days. Alex's ideas have been formed by some fairly conspicuous high-profile blunders. But really we need to study the reality of the whole situation, do we have statistics to back up the view that Mignolet is unreliable based on a couple of major wobbles? We would need to look at: shots saved, difficulty of shots saved, crosses taken, crosses missed, use of the ball when it's in his possession, goals conceded, number of goals conceded when it was conceivable he could have saved the shot, dealing with free kicks and organising the defenders in pressure dead-ball situations, his value in the dressing room and on the training ground, etc. From all of this data, it would then be possible to form a more objective view of the value of the player. Instead of which we remember a few blunders, which understandably stick in the mind, and because of that dismiss him as not good enough.

Now, I'm not saying one assessment is necessarily correct and the other incorrect, but what I am saying is that objectivity can really help when it comes to building up an effective squad of players. There are some really basic stats that are easy to get hold of these days, such as work rate, player responses to losing the ball in a challenge, running off the ball, tracking back, and so on. None of these are attributes in a player that spectators can easily monitor during the game.

Obviously, things aren't always that straightforward, and, of course, you don't always need stats to see the obvious. When Suarez was playing with Sturridge and Raheem Sterling at Liverpool, the three of them were clearly the best strike force in the Premier League and, at that point, Rodgers was seen as one of the best managers. Suarez and Sterling left, Sturridge got injured and — can you believe it? — Rodgers was soon out of a job. Check out Sturridge and Sterling's stats since that break-up and I bet they are nowhere near what they were. Suarez moved on to Barça where he joined Messi and Neymar, and another unstoppable strike force was created — no stats were needed to see that things went quite well for the three of them.

***

From our house it takes 50 minutes to get to Home Park and 50 minutes to get to St James Park (that's the one in Exeter, not Newcastle). So why did we end up supporting Argyle? Well, the first game that I went to with Josh was at Exeter. It was towards the end of the 1989/90 season, when Exeter won the Division Four title. I must say I was a bit shocked by the ground. Lots of rusty corrugated-iron sheeting, and a stand called the Cowshed. The feeling I got was really one of neglect. This was back in the '90s, things have improved since then.

In October of the following season we went to watch Argyle play Nottingham Forest in the League Cup. Forest were managed by the legendary Brian Clough and we got to see famous players like Des Walker, Stuart Pearce and Nigel Clough. We lost the game 2-1. I remember walking into Home Park and Josh's face lighting up. "This is more like it," I said to Sarah. We were standing in the corner next to the Mayflower Stand and facing the old Lyndhurst Stand. The stadium was all painted up in green and white and it really felt like the club was going somewhere.

At that time Argyle were managed by David Kemp, rumoured to be a long-ball merchant because of his previous job with the management team at Wimbledon. As a Liverpool admirer I was expecting the worst, but I don't remember ever thinking, "Oh my God, what the hell is going on here?" which is my usual response to watching route-one football.

Here I need to clarify the use of the term 'long-ball game'. When the long-ball game was first conceived, it was not – and still is not – just booting the ball up the park. Charles Reep, the guy who invented the tactic in the 1950s and called it 'direct football', worked out that most goals came after two or three passes, rather than after extended periods of possession. He tried to use statistics to prove that one long incisive pass up the field to cut out maybe 10 short passes was the most productive technique in terms of scoring goals. If you think about the season in which Leicester won the title against the odds, it's what they did a lot, and did really well.

It is actually a very beautiful way of playing the game. And then think about all the times we have watched Liverpool and Arsenal passing the ball around the edge of the area looking for that short, incisive pass to an amazing run into the six-yard box. Yes, stunning when it works out, but man, it so rarely does. And, so often from those prolonged periods of passing around the opponents' area, when the move breaks down and the break happens, a goal comes from that break. That long pass to Riyad Mahrez or Jamie Vardy, and bang, another beautiful goal, and so, so quick.

But back to Argyle. Halfway through the 1991/92 season Peter Shilton was appointed manager, and that was it, we went to every home game from then on. So many years of going to the football with Henry and Josh. I don't know what their memories of those days are, but mine are very sweet: Peter Shilton, Bruce Grobbelaar, Dan McCauley, Ivor Dewdney and Ginsters pasties, not very good tea in polystyrene cups and the sponsors Rotolok, what a glorious world to grow up in. I know if I was to ask Henry and Josh what is their very favourite memory of those years, it would definitely be the week we won the 50/50 and as I walked across the pitch to collect the money, the crowd saw my woolly hat and sang, "He's got a tea cosy on his head, He's got a tea cosy on his head." It felt good being in the old Division Two, and always the dream was there that somehow we might make it into the top flight.

***

The other day I was talking to Sarah about what it would be like to move into a city. Living out here on the moor is really nice, but it is pretty inconvenient for us at the moment because we have to drive into Exeter quite a bit. I was just wondering, you know, if we bought a house in Exeter would I drive down to Home Park, or would I just pop along to watch the 'Grecians'? Actually, that nickname has decided it for me — I would definitely drive down to Home Park. No, but seriously, Exeter City have some good things going for them. The thing I like most is that they are a community-owned football club; that counts for a lot in my book. But, realistically, what is the best that is going to happen to them? The most they can ever hope for is to be promoted into League One, and that's pretty unlikely. And, if they ever do get promoted, they will then face a relegation battle or two before returning to their rightful position in League Two.

On the other hand, with Argyle, I can see it is completely possible that one day we could play in the Premier League. Unlikely, I know, but all it requires is some belief from the owners of the club, and of course a large amount of luck. But the fact that it could happen is always there, and it is worth a lot. As many are prone to saying in regards to football: it's the hope that both sustains and kills you. It is a fact, sometimes disputed, that Plymouth is the largest city in England never to have hosted a top-flight football club.

1ST MARCH 2016, BARNET (A)

It is the morning of the match and everything is geared to getting the timing right for the journey. I definitely have time to get a couple of jobs done, and then I have to drive into town to buy a few supplies. My train leaves Exeter at 15.01, arriving in London at 17.24. That gives me a good 90 minutes to negotiate my way from Paddington to the ground. I need to be getting in my van around 13.30 to leave myself plenty of time to drive to Exeter, find a parking space and buy a parking ticket. Thankfully, I already have my train tickets. Ah, the joy of proper planning.

After lunch I'm ready to go. I grab my bag with everything in it, say goodbye to my wife and granddaughter, and hit the road. What can possibly go wrong now? I arrive at the station car park about 45 minutes early so I drive around a bit, just in case I can see a free parking space anywhere. I quickly realise that is not going to happen, so I head back to the car park. It's pretty full, in fact, there is one spare space and I just manage to squeeze the van into it. I write down my registration number because I know from experience that the machine requires it. I carefully watch the punter before me buy his ticket. And then it is my turn. I try to stay calm. Thankfully, there is no-one waiting in a queue behind me and I manage to buy my ticket without any trouble.

I get back to the van with the ticket and realise that I have bought it 35 minutes too early, so that, on my return journey, if the train is 20 minutes late my parking time will exceed the 24 hours I have paid for. I try not to think about it. I lock the van and set off to catch my train. As I get to the station entrance, I reach into my jacket for my wallet but it isn't there. I try all my other pockets and then I search my bag. I definitely don't have it with me. But I do have the piece of paper that I used to pick up the tickets a day earlier at Totnes station. I go to the ticket office and explain that I've left my wallet at home, and the guy says it is not a problem. But when he tries to print out the tickets, he realises I've printed them out once already.

"Sorry sir, it is absolutely impossible to reprint those tickets. There is no way that it can be done. The machine won't allow it."

Now I am getting a bit tense and wondering if my much-looked-forward-to away day is about to hit the skids. The ticket guy explains that the ticket I have does allow me to travel on any off-peak train, so I could get the next one, which leaves at 16.03. It arrives in Paddington at 18.21. There isn't time to drive home and pick up the tickets. If I can contact Sarah, and she can meet me halfway, then that might just work out OK. Getting to London at 18.21 makes it just about possible at the other end too. I phone Sarah and thankfully she is in.

"I don't have the tickets with me. Is my wallet there on the table?" I ask.

"Yes it's here," she replies. "I'll check to see if the tickets are here too. Yes, they are."

I explain that if she sets off right away, we can meet halfway and I will just have time to catch the next train. She grabs her car keys and tells me she is leaving straightaway. I rush back to the van and head back towards home. As I drive through Exeter, all the lights are green. The roads are clear and I relax into a kind of what-will-be-will-be state of being. I head out into the countryside and try to estimate where we will meet up. I work out that, ideally, we don't want to meet by passing each other on the road, and that the best thing to do is for me to turn around somewhere, park and wait for her to get to me. Actually, I work out that me driving towards Sarah doesn't save me any time at all, but it does save her some time so I press on.

At Dunsford I reckon our meeting up is imminent, so I turn around and park up. A minute later Sarah arrives. I grab my wallet and set off back to the station. As I pull into the car park, I wonder what I will do if there are no spaces. It is absolutely packed, but as I drive around, I see the space that I left is still there — and it is also the only free space available. I must have made some slight miscalculation on timing because I am now half an hour early for my later train. I have time to get a cup of coffee and relax. The Paddington train pulls into the station nine minutes late, not really ideal but never mind. I am on my way and things could have been worse.

I am lucky enough to get a good seat on the train by the window. Quite important for me, because I really enjoy just relaxing and looking at the view. I have a vague idea that I could sketch out a few ideas for the book, but to be honest the movement of the train makes it fairly difficult to type on the small screen of my phone. I begin to think about the origins of my obsession with football.

When we were young kids in the '50s my brother Phil had a 'New Footy' set. I'm pretty sure New Footy was an early incarnation of Subbuteo. (I've just looked on eBay and a 1950s set has recently sold for £49, I should have hung on to it.)

Anyway, Phil organised a League of six teams, and he then played out all of the games on the kitchen table. He picked teams with short names so that they fitted easily onto our blackboard. The two I remember are York City and, ironically, Exeter. I was the spectator and I loved it. The League Table was updated on the blackboard after every game.

We were both obsessed with football. We used to play for hours out on the lawn. It was a square of turf about 10 yards by 10 yards and at one end was a semi-circle of serious mud in front of the goal. The ball weighed a ton and it wasn't pumped up that hard. If you were unlucky enough to head in a cross, you really knew you'd done it, especially if you made contact with the laces. When it got dark Mum would call us in for a hot bath, and the water quickly turned to a deep chocolate-brown as all the mud dissolved off our legs and hands. We also used to go and watch Northleigh play in the Witney and District League. Sometimes we would go on the team bus to watch away games too.

The very first professional game of football that we went to watch was in 1959 at the Manor Ground in Oxford, the home of Headington United who played in the Southern League. I can't remember a thing about the game except that I got very, very cold. I remember walking from the ground to the bus station at Gloucester Green, and crying non-stop all the way because my feet were screaming with pain from the cold. I also remember that there was a lot of discussion about Headington United, soon to become Oxford United, because they were a non-League side of some quality but were unable to play in the League because there was no promotion and relegation system in place. At the end of every season, the bottom club in the League could apply for re-election, which happened every year without fail. But in 1962 Accrington Stanley failed to complete their fixtures, basically because of bad debts, and a vacancy arose which allowed Oxford United into the League.

As I remember it, the story of Accrington Stanley was quite a drama. They were one of the 12 teams in the League at its very beginning in 1888, and their demise was a very sad event. The club was re-formed in 1968 as Accrington Stanley FC and they climbed their way up the pyramid, eventually winning the Conference in 2006 and happily bringing League football back to the town. Ironically, the club that they replaced was Oxford United, who had finished bottom of what by then had become League Two.

In 1960 we moved from Northleigh in Oxfordshire to Padbury in Buckinghamshire. Our nearest League club was Northampton Town. Between 1960 and 1969 Northampton Town were promoted from Division Four to Division Three to Division Two and into Division One. They spent one year, 1965, in Division One, and then year by year were relegated right back down, ending up in Division Four in 1969.

In 1965 we did manage to get to the County Ground to watch a few games of First Division football, but I never for a moment thought of myself as a Northampton Town supporter.

I get off the train at Paddington. I have one big hurdle yet to cross — buying my ticket for The Tube. I find the Bakerloo Line no problem, but it soon becomes apparent that buying a ticket via a human is no longer possible. My war against the robots is about to continue. The options appear to be a choice of three machines: one that can take a debit card, one that can give change, and one that can't. (I have since found out that if you hold your debit card over those yellow blobby things you can pay for your journey that way. I am also certain, however, that if I had tried to do that it would have gone horribly wrong somehow.)

I have to be honest, I used to pride myself on the fact that I was a pretty cool dude, not much would stress me out, but as the years have gone by I'm now anything but, and I'd say the 'dude' part of the description is fairly questionable too. I begin to panic slightly.

A space becomes available at one of the machines that can take a debit card and I have no choice but to give it a go. I try to blank out of my mind the pressure I'm feeling from the people waiting behind me and start to follow the instructions. I type in Canons Park and for a while wonder why nothing's happening. Then I see that it is asking me for my pin number. Pressure, there's nothing like it to make you stop thinking. Thankfully, the number comes straight into my mind. I type it in and press the green button and phew, the precious ticket comes out. Another big hurdle passed.

The journey to Baker Street goes off without a hitch and now I am looking for the northbound Jubilee Line. I see a football supporter wearing a blue and white scarf and wonder if he is going to the match. I follow him for about 50 yards before I realise that there is a full League programme going on tonight, and that I have no idea what colour Barnet play in anyway. And then my luck changes. I see a supporter with a green and white scarf, surely that can only be Argyle. I follow him and he takes me all the way to the Jubilee northbound. Yes, it's nearly job done. I checked later and worked out that the blue-and-white scarfed supporter was probably on his way to watch Millwall play Wigan Athletic at the Den.

On the Jubilee northbound platform I introduce myself to the mystery Argyle supporter. He is a bloke about my age, or possibly a bit younger, called Phil. He lives in London and tries to go to as many away matches as he can. He tells me that he visits Plymouth about four times a year to see his dad, and as far as possible he tries to coincide the visits with home matches. I tell him that I live in Devon, near Moretonhampstead, and he asks me why I support Argyle and not Exeter. I explain what had happened and why we ended up as Argyle fans, and then he tells me he was born in Plymouth and when he was 10 years old his father took him to Home Park. From then on he was a regular in the Devonport End. He is a life-long Pilgrim. Let's face it, he was born a Pilgrim.

I start to think about my rootless existence as a football supporter, and my tenuous attachment to Plymouth Argyle. The first team that I truly supported in any way was Liverpool and I was born a million miles from there. And now I have this ridiculous attachment to the Greens, which does make a bit more sense because, at least geographically, we are in the same area. But what is it that makes me travel all this way for a 90-minute experience that has no guarantee at all that it will turn out OK? Why do I care whether Argyle win or lose?

The train arrives at Canons Park and I follow the crowd out of the station. There I meet Josh and a bunch of his friends, and we set off walking towards The Hive.

I do have a slight problem with ridiculous names in football. I recently went to the Bristol Rovers match with Josh and Henry and they had a stand there named The Dri-Build Stand. I suppose The Hive is not too bad as, after all, Barnet are nicknamed the Bees and they do play in gold and black stripes, you know, similar to bees. The thing is, which came first: the name or the look? Later, I tried to find out about the origins of Barnet's nickname and playing strip. I came across a great piece of trivia, which I have been totally unable to verify. According to some info about Barnet FC written on the Arsenal website in 2010, they were nicknamed the Bees because in the early 1900s the area around Underhill Stadium was known for its many apiaries.

But seriously, on the subject of naming stadiums and stands after companies, call me old-fashioned but I just don't like it. If they rename the Devonport End, the Dewdney's Pasty Stand, well, that could well be just enough to send me up the road to St James Park.

We get to the ground and find our way to the away section of the stadium. The Hive is a brand-new purpose-built stadium, opened in July 2013, and to be honest the whole place does feel a bit more like a facility than the home of a football club. Opposite the stand that we are in is what I presume are 'the other facilities': you know, corporate stuff, a gym and so on. If you were parachuted into The Hive without any information at all, facing the main building you could easily think that you had landed in the USSR. Lots of high brick walls with no windows, with a few rows of half-empty seats in front of them.

> On the plus side, our seats are spacious and very comfortable, and the refreshment facilities are really efficient. There is a bar with a huge telly in it, which is packed with punters. Josh and his mates are straight in there at half time and love it. I get myself a cup of tea and go back to my seat.

I know we have a new stadium too, but for comfort and facilities The Hive definitely beats Home Park hands down. I don't know a lot about football stadium design but I reckon you can buy stadia like Home Park off the peg. It feels like a generic design. You can probably order them in 'basic', 'standard' or 'deluxe', and Argyle have obviously gone for the basic. Nothing wrong with that I know, and certainly from the point of view of watching football matches the view is perfect with no seats with restrictions at all. Of course, I'm now talking about the new stands that surround 75 per cent of the ground. We still have the old Mayflower Stand, built in the early 1950s, with its cramped seats and the odd pillar obstructing the view. I've got to say though, it will be a shame to see it go. Surely, along with the glorious classic turnstiles, Home Park should be listed by now.

And while I am on the subject of architectural listing, on every man's bucket list should be a visit to the gents behind the Mayflower Stand. Talk about time travelling, these facilities will transport you straight back to the 1950s. We had urinals like that in our junior school in Padbury. They must have been built around the turn of the century. Half-round clay drains sunk in a concrete splash back, painted in black tar. A wholly inadequate flushing system that has probably not worked for years, and my oh my, what a smell. So much nostalgia for us oldies, and so much historical experience for the younger generation. They won't be there forever folks, so get along there soon.

Why do I reckon our new stadium is the basic model? Well, just look at the facilities and the area in which they are situated, it's all very, well, basic. Lots of concrete, very cold, and pretty unwelcoming. And, why, oh why does it have those really narrow, cramped new turnstile entrances? Actually, maybe that is what the majority of stadia are like. The old Wembley Stadium was certainly like that. I wonder what it is like at the Emirates and the Etihad. (By the way, do you prefer those names to Highbury and Maine Road? Because I don't.) The Hive does not give off a generic feel, but even so it does lack a bit of what you might call soul.

Do you know the worst thing about our new stand at Home Park? Obviously, and unless you are a regular there, you don't know this but you might be able to guess. The answer is — and I know it applies to a lot of other grounds too — even when there is only a medium-sized crowd, say around 7,000 or so, if you want a cup of tea at half time it will take you pretty much the whole of the break to buy it. About five minutes before the ref blows for half time, people start to surge out for tea, just to avoid those queues. That's a bit crap isn't it? And it wouldn't take much effort to put it right either.

So here I am at Barnet away. We have just about got settled in our seats and the match kicks off. I am pretty confident that over 90 minutes our superiority will pay off and we will return home with the three points. We have missed the team announcements, but it doesn't take long to see that we are playing with two strikers: Reuben Reid and Ryan Brunt. So we have two big strong guys up front, that sounds a bit of an ominous warning of the tactics we might be about to employ.

And here is the confirmation of how we are planning on playing: we are without our wingers, Greg Wylde and Craig Tanner. I am a bit surprised about leaving out Wylde. He has been pretty impressive in almost every game I have watched him play this season. I really like the way he unsettles defences by running at them. I reckon it is one of the most effective tactics a team can employ and we, the crowd, love it. Admittedly I haven't studied the stats, if they even exist, about how many of those runs turn into goals, but I think there is more to it than that. Psychologically, it puts a team on the back foot because it's difficult to find an effective way of dealing with a good winger.

The first 10 minutes of the game are a bit scruffy, to say the least. I spend most of the time hoping Argyle will settle down a bit. The pitch is really slippery and you can see the players worrying about keeping on their feet. After about a quarter of an hour, Jordon Forster, our defender on loan from Hibernian, skids head first into the advertising hoarding just along from where we're sitting. There is a really long delay as he has clearly injured his neck in some way. He is eventually stretchered off and the game restarts.

In no time at all Brunt is also stretchered off with a cruciate problem, so within the first 20 minutes we have two of our subs, Kelvin Mellor and Craig Tanner, already on the field.

The rest of the first half is fairly even. As nearly always happens to me, I am surprised at how good the opposition are. For some reason I always expect there to be a big difference in quality because of the League position, but actually most of the teams in the Division are pretty similar in standard. Of course, you nearly always get the odd stand-out team at the top. I was hoping it would be Argyle this season, but it turns out it's not. And you usually get the odd team or two that seem to have completely lost their way. This year it seems to be Dagenham & Redbridge's turn to play that role.

From quite early on it is clear that the danger man playing for Barnet is their no.9, John Akinde. He is a big strong guy who holds the ball up well and he is obviously a good footballer. Every time he gets the ball there is a bit of a feeling of 'oh no' among the Argyle supporters. Thinking he must be a player on the way up, at half time I take the opportunity to check his stats. Since making his professional debut in 2006, he has played for 11 clubs, all in the Conference, League One or League Two. His current spell at Barnet is by far his most successful, scoring 48 goals in 87 appearances.

Akinde's career interests me. He was first signed by Tottenham and, as it so cruelly says on his Wikipedia page, 'he failed to make the grade'. Aged 17, he began his playing career at Gravesend and Northfleet, playing in the Conference. In the following eight years he played just over 200 games, averaging around 25 a season, and he scored 40 goals. Since moving to Barnet at the age of 24 his career has suddenly come to life. As I mentioned earlier, he looks good to me. I wonder where his career will go from here. Could he be the next Ian Wright or Jamie Vardy?

Back to the match, and Tom, one of our mates, sitting directly behind me, manages to get a Green Army chant going in our section of the crowd. It takes some effort but he sticks with it and it pays dividends. I smile to myself as I remember back 20 years to when we played Fulham in the cup and won 5-0. We were sitting in the Lyndhurst and my son Henry valiantly started an "Are you watching Jimmy Hill?" chant that went right around the ground:

> *Are you watching?*
> *Are you watching?*
> *Are you watching, Jimmy Hill?*
> *Arrrrrre you watching, Jiiiiimy Hiiiill?*

Rest in Peace dear Jimmy. Not many people have made a positive difference in this world, but that three points for a win idea of yours certainly did.

***

Here at The Hive, at the end of the first half there are 14 minutes of added time due to the horrific injuries to our two players. It is all very tense, one of those games that could easily go either way. Not much of what I would call, 'quality football' and, to be honest, I am relieved when half time comes and the score is still 0-0.

Confident that the manager will settle the team down, I relax for the second half. And, true to form, we come out and have our best spell of the game. We are clearly the better team and it begins to feel like it is only a matter of time before we'll take the lead.

As is usual for Argyle, there is very strong away support. In a crowd of 2,209, 1,002 are Argyle supporters and they are very noisy. The terrace behind one goal is full of standing Argyle fans, and adjacent to that is a large seated area. We are sitting at the edge of it, up against the Barnet fans who for the most part are pretty quiet. They don't have a lot to cheer about really. I don't think our goalie Luke McCormick has had to make a save yet.

When we play at home I always like it if we can kick towards our own fans in the Devonport End in the second half. If we go behind, it feels like the support coming from the Devonport will really help even things up. Before we got the new stand, and the old Lyndhurst Stand was there, we always used to sit about two-thirds of the way along towards the away end. Then between the away fans and us there was always a very vocal bunch of fans who used to be constantly standing up, and who spent a lot of time goading the away supporters. We liked to sit quite near to them, but not too near, of course. We liked the atmosphere in that part of the ground.

Since the new stand has been built, that group of fans seems to have dispersed. Now, without doubt, the most vocal support in the ground comes from the Devonport End. They have a drummer too and sometimes the whole place really bounces. I now still sit in what would be the old Lyndhurst, but up at the other end to where we used to, because I enjoy being nearer to the Green Army, and because my best times at Argyle are when we are attacking the goal in front of our own fans.

And then, completely against the run of play, in the 69th minute Barnet score. God, that awful feeling. The ever-present near-certainty of Argyle being the better team and then going behind. I sometimes hate the injustice of football. Someone once told me that the reason they prefer watching rugby is that the game is not so much about luck as football is. The scores in rugby are more often related to the possession and the stronger team nearly always wins. I don't know if that is true, but I do know that so many times Argyle have been the better team but have then gone on to lose. And it's been the same with Liverpool this season too. Sometimes they have played sublime football but simply haven't had the run of the ball, and somehow the ball will just not go into the opponent's goal.

There are some situations in a match where it is completely down to luck which team ends up with the ball. In close tackles or when the ball is ricocheting around at close quarters, or — and I don't want to labour the point about long ball here too much — when the ball is hoofed up the park: who knows which team will end up with possession? Even from corners, I'd say it is pretty much impossible to cross a ball and successfully make contact with a specified player on your own side. There is a big slice of luck involved. That is why, if you watched the Champions League tie between Arsenal and Barça at the Emirates in February 2016 you will have seen the visitors taking loads of short corners. They must have worked out that keeping possession of the ball in that situation is at least as likely, if not more likely, to end in a goal, as banging the ball across into a goalmouth crowded full of players.

Of course I can understand the school of thought that believes that the nearer the ball gets to the goal, the more likely it is to go into it. And I can see why some spectators just want the ball moved in that direction as much as possible, but the proof of the argument has to be that when you watch the best teams in the world play, they simply don't do that. They play patient football, and when they get a chance to cut open the opponent's defence it is done very quickly and very efficiently. In rugby, territorial possession is what the game is all about. And, apart from the odd player who cuts through defences with dazzling runs, most of the scoring comes from pushing the other team back towards their own try line. Actually, maybe it doesn't. It probably comes from all the interminable penalty kicks given for all kinds of infringements beyond the understanding of the average man.

I'm prepared to live with the fact that luck is a big part of football. It makes the game more like life itself, and anyway, over a season, luck tends to average out. I'm not sure if I can say that over a lifetime luck tends to average out too. That would be a difficult point to argue.

Anyway, Barnet score. I'm not too bothered as there are still 20 minutes to go and we are clearly the better side. But again, I'm thinking about luck. If we had scored first, when we were so much on top, then the whole feeling of the game would have been different. We probably would have gone on to win the game by two or three goals, but as it is, they got lucky and now we are under pressure.

I secretly hope that, for once, we will stay calm and carry on playing the way we were. Of course, the psychology of the game has changed a bit now: Barnet are much more positive about things, and Argyle are beginning to show a slight air of desperation. We almost instantly revert to long balls and the nearer we get to the final whistle, the more we just boot the ball up the pitch. It's not a pretty sight.

But as long as it stays 1-0, there is always a chance of something. It's if it gets to 2-0, that's when it gets really hard to hold on to any hope.

The clock ticks by and it is beginning to look like the best we can hope for is a draw. It ticks by some more and then there are four minutes of added time. Then the final whistle goes and that's it, we are going home with nothing.

* * *

We slowly start to make our way to the exit. I catch the eye of another supporter and he claims some kind of victory for us because we have almost as many fans in the ground as they do. For a moment I feel proud to be a Pilgrim, and then I realise what I am doing. We lost, and really, I'm not sure having 1,000 fans there to see it counts as much compensation.

I make my way around to the club shop to buy a mug for my wife. After all, she did make it easy for me to take a day away so I feel buying her a mug in return is fair dos. I'm relieved to see that the shop isn't called 'The Barnet Retail Outlet', and that it is, in fact, just a nice little club shop. The young woman offers to wrap the mug in bubble wrap and puts it in a Barnet club bag. We chat about the game and I feel comforted by the warmth of respect between fellow football supporters. In younger years I would have assumed she just fancied me, but now I'm older I know that's clearly not the case and she is just a nice person.

There is something I really like about being in a crowd of people leaving a football match. The purposeful walking away from the ground, and the inevitable dodging of cars making their way out of the car park. Maybe it's the familiarity of the scene. I experience it after every match, and win or lose, it always feels good to me. There is the buzz of everybody talking about the game, and the analysis of the other results and the effect they have on our chances of promotion. My mind goes back to the first professional game I saw, at Manor Ground, and I feel grateful that my feet are not too cold. Leaving Home Park on a Saturday is also about getting back to the car to listen to *Sports Report* and maybe *606*. Here at Barnet, on a Tuesday night, it is about waiting a couple of minutes for our Uber to arrive. And then we relax and discuss the match on the drive back to Tower Hamlets.

Next morning, I am sitting in a cafe with Josh having coffee and toast for breakfast. We are discussing last night's football. Obviously not a great result for Argyle, but at least Yeovil won against Accrington, and good old Exeter drew with Portsmouth. Bristol Rovers had an emphatic win and it looks as if they are cranking up for a strong finish. Thankfully, because a couple of those results have gone our way, we are still hanging in there with a good possibility of automatic promotion. On the train home I plan to go through the remaining fixtures and make my predictions for the end of the season.

I mention to Josh that I spend a lot of time thinking about what appears to be the vast chasm between Division Two football and Premier League football. Why, for example, do Premier League players always look as if they have so much more time and space than is available in the lower League games? It all seems pretty obvious doesn't it? It has to be down to the skill levels of the players, that fraction of a second here, and the half-yard of ball control there, is clearly what makes the difference. That has to be true doesn't it? But I think maybe there is more to it than that. I determine to have a good think about the subject on the train home.

I have a couple of hours to get from East London to Paddington to catch the 12.06, so I'm feeling pretty relaxed about my journey. I tell Josh about yesterday's adventures with the train ticket, and that today, as long as my train is no more than 20 minutes late, my car park ticket will be fine. We decide to order an Uber so that I can catch the earlier train at 11.03. Ten minutes later I am sitting in the back of a brand new Toyota Hybrid on my way to Paddington station. Fifteen minutes later I am sitting in the back of a brand new Toyota Hybrid, a mile up the road from the cafe, completely stuck in a traffic nightmare.

My plan is to stay calm and enjoy watching London from the comfort of my cab. My driver, called Asif, has another plan. He wants to talk to me about Uber. It turns out that today is the start of his second week as an Uber driver. So far he is not doing so well. He explains how it works. Uber take 25 per cent of the fare. Then out of the remainder he has to supply his car, either rented, leased or bought. He has to pay a staggering £80 a week insurance, and he has to pay for the diesel. What is left is his wages. Last week, after expenses, he earned £4.50 per hour.

So far today Asif has had three £5 fares in an hour. So that's £11.25 for him, before expenses. Now he is taking me to Paddington, which should help a bit. We discuss the nature of Uber and the fact that it is a big gamble. When a possible punter comes up on his screen he has no idea what the job is, and when he accepts it, he has to follow through and do it. It could be rubbish or it could be a goldmine. But it's not really a goldmine because what's the best he can ever do? If he gets a job to Heathrow and makes himself £40, that's really only £30, and it's taken him a couple of hours. My driver is not going to get rich doing this.

Then there is the added complication of 'the surge'. The way Uber works is that if they need to attract drivers to a busy area, they increase the cost of the fares from that area; it's called a 'surge area'. If you are just outside a surge area you would ignore nearby calls and make your way to where the action is. It's a gamble. It seems to me that driving for Uber is all about playing the percentages, and to get that hourly rate up from £4.50 Asif is going to have to sharpen up his game.

And then at the end of the day, Asif needs to get back home to Newham. If he is in West London he could gamble on another fare, hoping it is going to go eastwards, but then he might end up back at Heathrow or even Gatwick. Or he could just accept that he now has to drive for an hour and a half using his precious diesel and not make a penny for it. I ask him how, as a Muslim, he feels about the gambling nature of his job. You see, I love to gamble. I don't mean at the bookies, I mean in everyday life. When I go on a call to look at tools I have no idea what I am going to find. When I open that toolbox it could contain a vintage plane worth £500, or a load of plastic-handled screwdrivers worth nothing. Asif admits he finds the gamble of it all is fun, and that he is fascinated by trying to play the game to his benefit. He realises that learning to be in the right place at the right time is the way to maximise his profits. I reassure him that as time goes on he will definitely get better at the game and therefore make more money. Asif is not so confident.

After about 15 minutes of going nowhere, Asif manages to take a right turn off the main drag and find his way on some back roads in what appears to be a westerly direction. It turns out that he used to be a minicab driver so he does pretty much know what he is doing. As we slowly wend our way through the maze of streets, the knowledge of his past experience gives me some hope that I might at least fulfil my original plans of catching the 12.06.

Our conversation now turns to what other options Asif has for making a living. He used to work in retail for JJB Sports, but when the company failed and the shop he worked in went down the pan, he couldn't find another job. In one vacancy he went for, he did manage to get to the last five being interviewed, but now in his forties he feels that his age goes against him. I have to say I have absolutely no experience of being in the jobs market, I have spent my life successfully avoiding that. I cannot imagine how trying and demeaning the interview process must be. I would have to be pretty desperate to put myself through that.

Somehow we manage to bypass the jammed-up traffic and we are now speeding along towards Paddington. We arrive with five minutes to spare to catch the earlier train. And the greatest thing about Uber is that you don't have to bother with cash or tipping, it all goes straight onto your account. I know a lot of people are freaking out about Uber but it surely has to be the way forward. So efficient, all they need to do now is make sure that the drivers can make a decent living out of it.

***

I make it to the train with a few minutes to spare and manage to find a good forward-facing seat with an unobstructed view. As soon as the train leaves the station, I make my way to the restaurant car and buy myself a coffee. I sit back and watch London pass me by. Could I ever live here? I always try to imagine what it would be like. I look at the flats with balconies and imagine the lives of the people who go about their day in them. At home I have sheds, and a yard, and a big garden. It would be a bit odd for me living without outside space. You know what, maybe I could get an allotment, that might work OK.

I go back in my mind to the question of the different skill levels in football. I remember watching junior school games where 20 kids in a pack chase the ball around the pitch. In a way, that is the ultimate route-one game — kick the ball towards your opponent's goal. There is very little space and time in those games. In terms of evolution, those young players must have eventually worked out that the odd pass, or probably what started out as an accidental kick towards another team member, is a more efficient way of making progress. I've never thought about this before, but when I was at junior school we played netball, which has zones on the pitch that the different positions are limited to. It was impossible to make any progress without passing the ball. I clearly remember our teacher telling us to pass the ball and then run into an empty space to receive the ball back again. I played at centre in some fiercely competitive games against other local schools. I loved that game.

Sitting opposite me is a lady, maybe in her late thirties. I'm thinking she is probably called Alison. She has her laptop open and is fiercely busy sorting something out. I don't know if I am allowed to say this, but Alison was obviously quite a looker in her day. I bet when she was in her teens she was what would be described in Blokeworld as a 'hot babe'. I do try not to spend huge amounts of time in Blokeworld — it can be quite unsettling — but I feel myself wanting to say to her, "ease back on the makeup, Babe". And then I realise that I still have this huge part of me that is what in the 1960s we called a sexist pig.

Alison is clearly some kind of executive or something powerful somewhere. Immaculately dressed and super organised, Apple logo proudly beaming out to the world, a pile of documents containing vitally important information by her side. We haven't gone far before her phone rings. Oh my, it's Jeremy.

Jeremy has some massive dilemma with a letter that he has to send out to one of their clients. It turns out that they work in the finance department and Jeremy's job appears to be chasing up late payments. He seems very nervous about something and is keen to get some help from Alison. She tells him at least three times that when he has written the letter, he should take it upstairs to Hugh in the legal department. Hugh is apparently very good and very easy to talk to. After about 10 minutes it really begins to feel as if what needs to be said has been said, but then Alison tells him one more time to chat with Hugh. She makes sure that Jeremy knows exactly who Hugh is: he sits in the corner, upstairs, and again she reassures him that he is easy to talk to. And then it's over, and she's back on the laptop.

My mind wanders back to football and my obsessive dislike of the long ball. I don't think I have ever been to an Argyle game where, at some point, the ball hasn't just been hopefully kicked up the park. And every time it happens, without fail, I wonder if there was something else the player could have done that would have been more profitable. Of course, I accept that sometimes the pressure is so great that the kick up the park is the best option available, but quite often there are also the options of passing the ball to another player, or keeping possession.

When the ball is kicked up the park, even roughly in the direction of another team-mate, most times possession is lost. The way I see it is that the defending team have a huge advantage in that situation because they are naturally facing the ball coming towards them, and it shows. Of course there are the odd times when the ball breaks in favour of the attacking team, and there are the odd times goals get scored. But this happens quite rarely.

I have sat in the stands at Home Park for many years now, and I am quite familiar with the emotions of the Argyle fans. There is quite a high percentage of fans who do appreciate the ball being booted up the park, and there are always some terrible moans of despair when what you might call 'possession passes' go astray or get intercepted by the opposing team. There is no doubt that there is a strong feeling in the crowd that the nearer to the opponents' goal the ball gets, the more likely it is to go in. Let's face it, the logic of that statement is almost overwhelming.

I have to put my hands up now and admit that I have no statistics to back up my argument. Maybe all I have on my side is the fact that I enjoy watching good football. There is also the fact I have already alluded to: that the most successful teams in the world play possession football.

And that leads me to the question I have been thinking about on the terraces at Argyle for many years. At what point when you descend the pyramid of football skill does it become profitable to play the long ball game? I remember in the late 1980s Wimbledon had a run of success in the old First Division and then in the 1990s they were very successful in the newly formed Premier League. During those years many people put forward the argument that a team like Wimbledon doing so well was the final evidence that the long ball philosophy was correct. I remember reading headlines like 'The death of football' and 'No need to pass'. Since Wimbledon's demise that discussion has dropped away, and nowadays it is a pretty much accepted fact that at the top levels of football the passing game wins out.

About five minutes before we are due to pull into Taunton station, Alison shuts down her Apple and begins to pack things away. As the train pulls into the station, she stands up and puts on her coat. She is a master of timing, obviously having done this journey many times before. I need a break from deep thought, so I decide to study the passengers walking up and down the platform. Actually, that last sentence should read: "I am a nosey sod, so I am looking out of the window passing judgment on a bunch of people I know absolutely nothing about." And then I see Alison walking towards me. I can't work out if she lives in London and has someone to visit in Taunton, or she works in Taunton and today she has had a meeting up in London. Then I think of Hugh, upstairs in the legal department, in the corner, who is very easy to talk to. Yep, I think that's where she is heading right now judging by the spring in her step.

***

I spend the rest of the journey thinking about how to work out my predictions for the final League positions based on current form. I am going to take the points total of the last six games for each of the teams in the Division. Then I will make a League Table based on that. And then I'll go through the remaining games of the season allocating points depending on the position of each team in my mini League: three points if you are clearly better than your opponent, and one point if you are on the same points or one point above or below your opponent. That all sounds fairly simple, I can do that in front of the telly.

We pull into Exeter station bang on time and I try to replicate Alison's cool descent. I panic almost immediately when a couple of passengers have to wait as I struggle to put on my coat. I apologise for getting in their way, and sort of slide back into my seat space to let them by. Is that bad timing or simply a lack of self worth? To be fair, Alison didn't have the pressure of the other passengers bearing down on her, but secretly I feel that even if she had, she was secure enough within herself to ride it out.

I get to the van with a good hour to spare, open the back door to make sure the tools are all still there, which they are, and so now here we go, the final leg of the journey. Well, not quite. I have to stop at the shops in Cowick Street to buy my granddaughter a cake. I know it's the first thing she will ask me for when I walk through the door.

***

It's Wednesday afternoon and I'm back on the moor thinking about getting ready for market this Friday. The forecast is shit, which is nothing new, we've just come through the wettest winter I can remember. After five years of trading outside in the open air I have finally bought a stall, so at least now I am partially guaranteed a bit of dry. I decide to clean a few tools and load them into the van. I'm not in the shed long before I hear Alex approaching. I really could do with not standing around talking for too long this afternoon.

"Hi mate, how are you?" I ask.

"Good thanks, Tom. How was the match?"

"Well, you know, we lost, but it was fun. Funny thing is, these days I don't take losing as badly as I used to."

"Ah yes, you must be getting philosophical in your old age I guess."

"What are you up to today Alex?"

"Oh, just messing about here and there. I need a good strong chain to pull a dead tree out from a hedge. Have you got anything that might do it?" "You can borrow this if you want" I say as I hand Alex my best tow-chain, "But make sure you put it back. I definitely don't want to lose it."

"Yep, no problem," says Alex. 'I've got my mate coming around in a minute. If I'm not about can you send him down my way?"

"Of course I can," I say, wondering if we are going to get away without an extended football conversation this afternoon.

"You know when you go and watch lower League football?"

Ah, here we go, just like clockwork.

"Yep," I say.

"Well, when you come back and then watch the Premier League on telly, do you think, blimey, what a difference?"

That makes me smile a bit.

"Ha, it's funny you should ask that, because that's exactly what happens to me, every single time. It's hard to believe that in the great spectrum of football, there can be such a difference between the elite of the Premier League and just three levels below them in League Two."

"Yes," says Alex, getting more and more animated by the second. "And why, in the Premier League, does there always seem to be more room on the pitch, and why do the players seem to have so much more time?"

I can see that Alex is going to settle in for a long discussion, not that I really mind because this is something I have been interested in for years. The obvious answer about increased skill levels giving the top players more time and space comes into my mind but I keep quiet, hoping that Alex might come up with some new ideas of his own.

And then he says, "Oh shit, I'd better go. I've left the tractor down the field with the engine running." He grabs the chain and is gone. For a few minutes I carry on thinking about all the reasons why the Premier League looks so classy compared to League Two.

I thought about the gang of kids in school chasing the ball around the field, and how the good players look for spaces. A couple of games ago I noticed that our left-back, Peter Hartley, had started to drift out wide whenever our goalie, Luke McCormick, got the ball. Several times in quick succession, McCormick threw the ball out to him in lots of space and some quite promising moves were starting to develop from there, so much more promising than the alternative long hoof up the park.

If you have several players looking for space, to that degree, it is going to change the quality of the game, and, of course, it is going to give the impression of more time, because it creates more time. It's obvious stuff I know, but if it is so obvious why don't teams do it as standard? They would probably argue that they do, and I'm sure to a degree that's true. I think the big difference is that the lower League teams could easily play good football but often they just don't have the courage to risk it. The problem is that when it goes wrong, it can be very costly. Losing possession in your own half really sets off the alarm bells. Far safer to get the ball up the pitch and hope to get lucky with gaining possession in a safer area of the field.

There is a knock on the shed door and it is Alex's mate.

"Hi, I'm James and I'm looking for Alex."

"Ah OK, he's down the field, James. Wander on down, no problem."

"OK thanks, I will. I'm guessing you must be Tom. Alex has told me he has some interesting chats with you."

I laughed at that. "I guess we do," I say. "But interestingly they are always about the same subject."

"Now then," says James. "Let me guess. Would that subject be football?"

"Yep, that's right," I reply.

"I'm guessing Alex has never gone into why he always talks about football then, has he?"

"No, never mentioned anything about it really. We did have a good conversation once about how blokes use talking about football to avoid talking about other stuff. I had to agree with him on that one, because I do that all the time myself. I mean, Alex clearly loves football, and he does seem to know a lot about it. So are you telling me that there is more to this than meets the eye?"

"Oh God, there certainly is," James replies.

Just then Alex arrives back up from the field. "Oh hi, James," he says.

"Hi, Alex. How are you doing today mate?" asks James.

"Good thanks, I heard your car come into the yard. Do you want to come down the field with me for a bit while I quickly finish this job, then we can go and have some tea?"

"Sure, no problem. I might see you later, Tom," says James as they disappear out of the door.

Wow, I'm left standing in the shed pondering on that one: "I wonder what that is all about?" I catch myself talking to myself out loud, which I'm pretty sure is something I rarely do.

It's Wednesday evening and Sarah is watching some intense detective drama on the telly. The deal is that I get the best seat by the fire and she gets to choose what's on. Over the years I have learned to shut the telly out of my mind almost entirely. Occasionally, if it gets really grim I say something along the lines of "Oh my, this is a bit full on isn't it?" There is never a reply, but she does usually shunt the volume down a notch or two to help me on my way.

I'm pretty tired, so I decide to play a game of Go online. Go is a Chinese board game that I have been playing for years. I am a fairly average player. I suppose in football terms I'd be 'middle of the Conference with no hope of ever being any better' kind of level. Even now I still think I could improve my game if it was my only goal. But it's not. Go has been relegated below even the flower garden these days. It is little more than a bit of relaxation at the end of the day for me now.

But maybe there are still lessons to be learnt from what is no doubt a beautiful game. The other day when I was at the home education group with my granddaughter, I was playing chess with one of the older kids there and I couldn't believe what a clunky game it is compared to the beautiful flowing experience of playing Go. How I approach the game very much depends on my mood. If I am what might be described as 'slightly out of it', then I just press the 'Find an Opponent' button and start throwing stones around the board without much thought. I might try stuff I have never tried, I might try to start fights straightaway, or I might deliberately ignore my opponent's moves. Occasionally — and I don't do this often because it is a horrible thing to have happen to you — I might mirror my opponent's moves. Then after a while, if I am still in the game, I settle down and start to play more seriously.

Sometimes I am in a more reflective state of mind. Before I start a game, I give myself a little pep talk (not out loud) about what I am going to try to achieve in this particular game. I try to encourage myself to see and play a bigger game. I know that I need to look at the whole board, and I need to try to play moves that keep the game in the balance so that I don't find myself in the all-too-familiar position of playing to claw back a game I have already lost. A few months ago, I managed to maintain a sound mental approach to the game over an extended period of time and I actually got promoted to the heady grade of 3 kyu. I photographed the screen because I knew it wouldn't last, and sure enough it wasn't long before I was back down at 5 kyu, surely my true Go home, a bit like Exeter and League Two. (Yes, I know that is a cheap shot even by my standards, but this is a book about football so I do have to try and tie everything together with the common thread, and look, there it is.)

But the point I wanted to make about Go and how it relates to football is this: although I know what I have to do to improve my grade, and although to a degree I can actually do it, for some reason I don't. I choose to play a smaller game or I choose to get into scrappy little fights, instead of choosing what I need to do to become a better player. And sometimes, when I play a small move, my opponent thinks for a bit and comes up with a mighty move that shows his big intentions. And I am drawn up short, and left to ponder my small-minded outlook. At that point, if I am lucky, and it's not too late, I can refocus my mind onto the larger game and save the day.

Now I am wondering, is that the same in the lower levels of football? I think to an extent it is. We do get drawn into less grandiose ways of playing the game. Certainly we don't trust our ability to play our way out of difficult situations. We rely on chance much more. We gamble on our opponents making mistakes, and we minimise the chances of our own mistakes being made in vital areas of the pitch by booting the ball away from them.

And what happens if we come up against a team that plays a bigger game? The first thing we do is try to make them play on our level. I saw this in reverse when we played Wycombe at home earlier this year. It was horrible. We were on a good run of form and my hopes were sky high. We had been playing some lovely football and I was saying things along the lines of, "This is the best Argyle team I have ever watched". Then Wycombe turned up, and they were a big physical team. They had no interest in playing football. They just took the game down to their level. It was messy, it was hard, it was almost scary, and they won 1-0.

Now could we have done anything about that? I really don't know the answer to that question but that match, in lots of ways, was the turning point of the season for me. It feels like that was the point at which we began to lose a bit of faith in playing good football. We still try, of course, but there always appears to be just that slight lack of faith in the belief that good football will always win out.

5TH MARCH 2016, OXFORD UNITED (H)

It's Thursday morning and we've got Oxford United at home on Saturday. It's a crucial match because they are second in the League and we need to stay in touch. My confidence levels are low. In fact, I'm dreading it. I've asked Alex to give me a hand with a bit of landscaping that I have been working on for the last few months. I really need to get it finished now. The weather is perfect so I am hoping to get a good day's work in. While I potter about waiting for him to turn up, I wonder if I will be able to get any info out of him concerning his infatuation with the subject of football. I am certainly planning to give it a go.

"Oh hi there, Alex. How's your day been so far?"

"Good thanks, Tom, and yours?"

"Yeah, good mate. Looking forward to getting this work finished. It's been bugging me for a while now."

The thing about Alex that I really like is that when it comes to working, he just plugs away at it. He doesn't go too fast and he keeps going at it until it is right. If something needs to be changed, you can just tell him and he simply gets on with changing it. So as the day goes on the project begins to take shape. It looks really good and I begin to imagine what it will be like once Sarah has put a few plants in place.

It has been an interesting experience for me doing this job. It is the most ambitious project I have taken on for years. I am pleased, and also relieved, that it has turned out as well as it has. I can see already that it has achieved its aim, which is to encourage people to walk through the garden to get to the veg garden and polytunnel, rather than walk on the road. God, when you put it like that it sounds like an awful lot of time spent to achieve a very small aim. There are a lot of other benefits too: better views, more light, a garden for our granddaughter to play in, and somewhere nice for us to hang around in. I imagine a few of my closest friends here on a sunny afternoon, talking and having a laugh. It probably won't ever happen. I am socially very lazy, and I'm sure Sarah won't mind me saying, she is too. We never make any effort to do anything much in that area of life.

But you know, maybe if this garden starts to look really good, I will be inspired to send out the invitations. I mean, it's not like when I was young and I was too frightened to invite girls out in case they said no. I'm pretty sure I've got a few friends now, or at least Sarah has, who would actually say yes because they wanted to come, not just because they felt that they had to. I mean to say, it's not going to turn into one of those nightmare scenarios where you finally drum up the courage to ask the girl out, and she says, 'yes', and then when you get to the actual date you realise she only said yes so she could hang out with your best mate. God, I'm sometimes glad I'm past my sell-by date, but then I do admit there are other times when I wouldn't mind giving the whole thing another go around.

The biggest part of this landscaping job, or perhaps I should say, the most crucial part, was digging out the bank to set the level of the lawn. I wanted to make it so that the garden invited you to walk across it. I know that sounds very Charlie Dimmock, and pretentious beyond words, but it isn't really. I needed to create the thought that if I want to walk to the polytunnel, then this is the path I need to take. It was a very practical aim. The problem came when I decided that I could move the gateway at the far end of the lawn, which would then allow me to take the level of the lawn even lower. Of course, by then it was all a little too late because I was reluctant to change all the work I had already done.

I suffer from a common human condition in that everything that I do, I can always see more that can be done. I am forever doomed to utter the words, "OK, that will have to do". When I am writing I sometimes come away thinking, "hmmm that could have been better," or even worse: "hmmm I'll leave that to the editor to sort out". And then later, I read it through and most times it's actually just about OK. I often wonder if I will ever settle down and finish a job to the point where there is no more improvement to be made. Is that even possible? Maybe today I will go out into the shed and restore a plane to the point where I can see nothing else that I can do to it. Why do I even say these things when I know I will never do them?

And now I am drifting into the world of economics, which often happens because it is a subject that fascinates me. Over the last 50 years, I have worked out that it simply is never worth doing a job perfectly. For example, if I'm working on a Stanley no.4 plane, which at the end of the day I can sell for between £12 and £20 at best, and if I value my time at £10 per hour (which in the real world I don't because my time is priceless, but in the world of planes I do) then for that Stanley plane, the most time I can give it is 30 minutes. So in that particular case, to do that job properly, I have to get that plane to a saleable condition in as short a time as possible. Doing the job properly is nothing to do with perfection. It is to do with putting in the minimum amount of effort to make the maximum amount of profit. And that dear reader, is why I am not politically of the right. There just has to be more to life than making a profit.

We've gone all day working on this garden and we've hardly spoken to each other. For a while I have been wondering how I can approach the subject of Alex's obsession with football. And then suddenly, out of the silence, he speaks.

"Tom, I bet you can't guess what I have been mostly thinking about today. In fact, if you guess correctly, I will give you this day's work for free, but if you guess wrongly, then you pay me double."

"Whoa, that's a bit of a big wager for me, Alex. I'll tell you what, if I guess wrongly, in return I will help you with this week's Super 6 entry for free. How's that for a deal?"

"Done," says Alex.

"So do you mean guess the subject, or do you mean guess the actual line of thought?" I start. "Because clearly the subject is going to be football, and secondly the line of thought is concerning whether Liverpool will make it into Europe next season."

I sense that we are finally moving towards my goal.

"Ah well, you are wrong there on both counts," Alex replies, "because actually today I have been mainly thinking about music. I have been wondering if each human being on the planet has a basic rhythm in their body that attracts them to one form of music or another."

I can't resist laughing, partly because it is such a ridiculous idea that a 40-year-old bloke could spend most of the day thinking about that, and partly because it is something that I have also thought about many times, but never for longer than about two minutes at a time.

"Do you know what, Alex? Even though that is a very interesting subject, and something that I accept you have thought about today, I don't believe you when you say it is the main thing that you have thought about today."

"No, Tom, you're wrong there. It is the main thing that I have been thinking about, I promise."

"But come on, Alex, you only ever think about football. Are you honestly telling me that you have thought more about this rhythm thing than about football? I'm struggling to believe you."

"What do you mean, I only think about football? That's ridiculous. I am a well-rounded individual who can converse on a wide variety of topics." Alex is laughing now, and I am steeling myself to go in with the big question.

Except that he beats me to it. "Ha, so you really started to think that I have been thinking about the core rhythm of the human being there, didn't you, Tom?"

Alex is still laughing. He is pretty pleased with his little stunt. I have to admit it was quite clever. "OK, I'll tell you what I have really been thinking about now, shall I?"

"Yeah, and at the same time I will enjoy how much work I've got done for free today. Go on then, tell me."

"Well, Tom, I have been working on this project in the evenings. It's to do with Super 6. Next season, I am going to enter another character into the competition who is going to make all his choices based on luck, and I am going to see if he beats the selections that I make based on my football knowledge."

"Good one, Alex. I like that idea very much," I reply, and I actually do; chance against knowledge, interesting idea.

"So I've put a lot of thought into this and I've now started to make the spinners that will make the selections.

I'm trying to make it so that the element of luck is based on actual statistics. I have counted up the scores for the last three seasons, in terms of home wins, away wins, and draws, and I am counting up the total numbers of different amounts of goals scored by each team in every game of the season. So for example, there will be a total of zeros and a total of ones and so on, which I will then work out as percentages and put on a pie chart. Then I will put this data onto the spinners, one spinner for the home team and one for the away team, and I have decided to divide the spinners into four sections and reproduce the info in each section to minimise the likelihood of distorting the results by having an unbalanced spinner."

"You've really thought this through haven't you, Alex?" I'm not sure whether I am feeling awe or pity for this guy by now. I think the former, but it could edge toward the latter dependent on how the next minute or so goes.

"Oh yes, I'm determined to do this properly," says Alex. "I've also decided that I won't have crazy scores like 6 or 7 because they are very rare, and, to be honest, if a team scores six or seven, or even five, it doesn't affect the result does it? They are always going to be the winning team. Obviously, you are going to get the odd incorrect score by not using those numbers, but it would be really difficult to divide the spinner to show the tiny amount of times that sixes and sevens are scored."

Oh my God, this guy is seriously into this. I am torn between my own fascination with this kind of stuff and my built-in wariness of not getting too involved in these kinds of areas of life for fear of people taking the piss out of me. I can feel the potential for heartbreak and my instinct is to flee when I feel that around the place. But out of politeness I feel I have to carry on.

"So, Alex, how are you going to make these spinners then? Because there is going to be a big chance they will rig the results, isn't there?"

"Well no, not really, Tom. See, I am making them out of wood."

Phew, that's something, I think to myself. For a minute I was imagining these kind of cardboard things with biro-marked divisions and bent cardboard needles spinning on pins.

"I've given this a lot of thought," Alex continues. "I've already made the bases of the spinners and I've incorporated two-way levels into the edges of them. They lie flat, see. And I've sunk a bearing into the middle so that the needle spins freely. The needle will be perfectly balanced. There won't be any inaccuracy."

"Wow, it all sounds really good Alex," I say, just about believing myself. "I'd love to see the spinners when you have finished them."

"No problem Tom. I'll bring them over to show you."

This is not the moment to start a conversation with Alex about his obsession with football and the causes of that obsession. I kind of know Alex is an interesting guy in a way that I can't put my finger on, but now that I have had a glimpse into his world, my mind is trying to pin all sorts of labels on him.

We carry on working quietly towards the end of the day.

My mind takes me back many years to when we had a lodger in our attic. He was around 30 years of age. He was a nice enough guy, not my cup of tea but then few are. He was always polite, paid his rent, and was quiet enough — all you need from a lodger really — but I always thought he was a little odd. Then one day I had to go up into the attic while he was at work. It was a strong policy of mine that I didn't invade other people's space unless I really had to, but in this case I desperately needed to turn off the water for a few minutes to mend a serious leak. I unlocked the door and walked into the flat, and there, all over the floor, were roads made out of cardboard boxes with pencil lines for road markings, and a few toy cars in car parks, and a couple of small boxes turned upside down, which I imagine were buildings.

That day my mind went into overdrive with the search for labels too. Now, looking back, I think what the hell? Really it's no different to the crazy stuff I do is it? I mean, why build a garden? Why collect hand tools? Why get excited when I see a rare bird? Why follow football? Why build spinners with levels and bearings to predict football results? The list is endless. Yes, human beings are a strange creation aren't they? And, blow me, guess what? I am one of them, and so are you!

> "You don't fancy coming to the match with me tomorrow do you, Alex? It's going to be a pretty exciting game," I ask, as Alex is packing up to go home.
>
> "Ooooh no, I couldn't do that I'm afraid. Anyway, James is coming round tomorrow and we're going to finish off some work I'm doing on my tractor."
>
> "Ah, OK," I say, "I might see you in the morning then before I go. Goodnight then, and take care."

It's amazing how things can change. Six weeks ago we were top of the League. We played Northampton at home in a Tuesday evening fixture at Home Park in front of 10,000 fans. It was an even game that we could so easily have won, but we lost. Northampton are now flying at the top of the table and we are left looking over our shoulders trying to work out if we can avoid the play-offs. Today we face Oxford who, after we lost at Barnet, are one place above us in second place on goal difference. This is a big, big game!

That game against Northampton was one of those games which, had it gone our way, would have almost certainly made a dramatic difference to the way our season played out. At the time it didn't seem like a disaster. We had won our previous four games and everything was looking good. You don't expect to win every game, and 12 points from 15 is good by any standards. But crucially, it was the game where we lost top spot. Since then, top spot has been slowly slipping into the distance and the focus has now become automatic promotion, or for the layman, finishing in the top three.

As usual on a match day, my mind is focussed on what time I need to get in the car and make my way to Home Park. I make sure that any jobs I get involved in are not urgent and they must have the minimum chance of turning into a nightmare. For example, it would not be a good time to begin a plumbing project, whereas cleaning out the car or tidying up the recycling are perfect.

I decide to check the tyre pressures on the van, and maybe clean the windscreen. It's just gone 11 and I wonder what the players are up too right now. What time do they all get together, and when do they find out if they are playing or not? The other day I was watching Liverpool on telly and I saw Christian Benteke on the bench. I'm sure he is earning a fortune but he looked pretty pissed off about not playing. There are some really good players who never actually play. Reserve goalies for example. The top clubs must have some of the best goalies in the world and just keep them there as back-up. I have to say I'd struggle with that a bit. If I had decided to be a professional footballer and then I couldn't get a game, I'm not sure the money would really make sense of that situation for me. I do feel for the squad members who just hang around not playing, watching their bank balances grow as their lives go by.

***

I can hear a car coming up the road. It sounds like an old Land Rover. More than likely it is James coming up to help Alex with his tractor. If it is, I wonder if I will get a chance to hear the rest of the story that I missed out on the other day.

Yes, sure enough my engine recognition skills are bang on. It's James in his smoky old tdi200. I used to love that engine until my conscience about the environment got the better of me. Crazy really, because I sold my Land Rover but it's still driving around, it's just that it's not me driving it. I might as well have kept it for all the difference that sale made to the health of the planet.

"Hi, James. How are you this morning? See you're still struggling on with that old Land Rover," I say.

"Yep, all good here, Tom," James replies. "And yep, I love my old Land Rover, and no, I'm not going to let it go any time soon."

"So, James, listen. The other day you were about to tell me about Alex's obsession with football, and then we got interrupted. Have you got a minute now to fill me in on that?"

"Sure I have," says James. "It's pretty simple really."

I was all ears, at last the mystery was about to be unveiled.

"The thing is, Tom, Alex is one of those blokes who was born really good at football. In school, whichever side he was picked to play for, that side always won," James begins.

He goes on to tell me an incredible tale. Alex was head and shoulders better than any of the other kids in the area. He soon got spotted by a local club, which James refused to name. Anyway, he rose up through the ranks, always getting his deal renewed at each age level. Gradually they go through the kids they have selected, until it starts to get a bit serious as they are approaching the kind of age where they can make a decision about whether to make football a career or not.

There just never seemed to be any doubt that Alex would become a professional footballer. Everyone just assumed that was what was going to happen. And then, when he got to 17, suddenly he was told by the club that they were going to let him go. What happened next was just terrible. Alex had a complete meltdown. Maybe you might call it a nervous breakdown or something like that. No-one saw him for ages. He just stayed at home in his bedroom, and no-one knew what was going on. The next thing anyone heard was that Alex had been arrested, actually in the football stadium of the club he was signed to, and that he had been caught smashing the windows of the executive boxes.

"As it turned out," James finishes, "the club decided not to press charges, and someone managed to persuade Alex that he needed to get some help. This he did, and some months later, he quietly started to appear around the place again, doing this and that. Since that time, and that's over 20 years ago now, Alex has never ever played football again. But as you can tell, he is still utterly obsessed with the beautiful game."

'Wow," I say. "That's quite a story. I wonder why he just gave up playing like that? You would have thought he would sort of look around for other opportunities, wouldn't you?"

My mind is racing at this point, finally a full answer but still questions everywhere.

"Well yes, that's what we thought he should have done," James continues, "but I guess he thought if he wasn't good enough for a lower League club, where the hell could he go from there. He had dedicated his whole life to being a footballer, and the thing is, he almost made it. But you know what's really bad? Or maybe it isn't. When the club decided they didn't want him, it was just bye-bye without a second thought."

"Thank God they didn't press charges," I say. "He could have come out with a criminal record as well as a broken heart, couldn't he? Still, he seems OK now doesn't he?"

"Yeah, he's OK now. Credit to him. He's quietly got on with his life and he's a nice enough guy isn't he?" says James. "He's my best mate anyway."

I decide to press on a bit with my investigations.

"You know yesterday, James, I asked Alex if he wanted to come to Home Park with me today."

"Yep, don't carry on, Tom. He said no didn't he? He has never been to a football ground anywhere since he had that meltdown. And I think it's only because he's scared the whole thing is going to come flooding back into his mind. I think he thinks, he got through a difficult spell there and he's going to play it pretty carefully because he doesn't want the wheels to come off ever again. Seriously, I think that's all there is to it."

"Well, cheers for that, James. And I promise I won't breathe a word of it to anyone." And as I say those words I think to myself, wow, what a story. Goes to show that sometimes you can know someone and yet still not understand the things that have defined their life to that extent. Amazing.

***

I set off on my journey to Home Park bang on time. I find my usual parking space and take my usual walk through Central Park. I check to see if there is a new fanzine out, then go through the turnstile into the ground. I buy my cup of tea and find my way to my favourite seat, where I wait for the match to begin. I think quite a bit about Alex. I guess there are lots of kids who want to be footballers and who don't quite make it. For me, well of course I wanted to be a footballer too, but — do you know what? — I knew from pretty early on that was never going to happen.

***

We draw with Oxford 2-2. We're still on for automatic promotion, but there's a long way to go. Remember, anything can happen in football, and, oh yes, can someone please tell me, is it just supporting Argyle that is a tough gig, or is it the same with every team?

PART TWO

SHAME ABOUT THE RESULT

So, to my League Two predictions. Here's the League Table the day after Barnet away – top 10 positions:

		P	PTS
1	NORTHAMPTON TOWN	34	75
2	OXFORD UNITED	34	64
* 3	PLYMOUTH ARGYLE	34	64
4	ACCRINGTON	32	56
5	PORTSMOUTH	33	53
6	BRISTOL ROVERS	33	53
7	LEYTON ORIENT	34	53
8	WIMBLEDON	33	52
9	WYCOMBE WANDERERS	33	52
10	MANSFIELD TOWN	34	51

And here's my predicted finish based on the form of the previous six games:

		P	PTS
1	NORTHAMPTON TOWN	46	109
2	OXFORD UNITED	46	96
3	ACCRINGTON	46	91
* 4	PLYMOUTH ARGYLE	46	80
5	WIMBLEDON	46	79
6	MANSFIELD	46	77
7	PORTSMOUTH	46	69
8	LEYTON ORIENT	46	69
9	WYCOMBE WANDERERS	46	67
10	BRISTOL ROVERS	46	66

Finally — and spoilers here — this is the actual League Table at the end of the season:

		P	PTS
1	NORTHAMPTON TOWN	46	99
2	OXFORD UNITED	46	86
3	BRISTOL ROVERS	46	85
4	ACCRINGTON	46	85
5	PLYMOUTH ARGYLE	46	81
6	PORTSMOUTH	46	78
7	WIMBLEDON	46	75
8	LEYTON ORIENT	46	69
9	CAMBRIDGE	46	68
10	CARLISLE	46	67

(* marker beside row 5, PLYMOUTH ARGYLE)

30TH MAY 2016, WEMBLEY

So, what about my idea that maybe you can predict the end of season results from studying the form three-quarters of the way through the season? Well, basically, you can't make that prediction reliably, because form can change at any time. In this instance, Bristol Rovers' end to their poor mid-season form coincided with the beginning of my survey, and their predicted finish in 10th place proved to be hugely wrong. On the last day of the season, they moved into third place with a winning goal in the 92nd minute against Dagenham & Redbridge. The very last goal scored in the League Two 2015/16 season brought them level on points with Accrington but ahead on goal difference, giving Rovers third place and automatic promotion.

Conversely, with Mansfield, who I had down as a form team to finish in the play-offs, their form dropped right off and they failed to even finish in the top ten, just managing to finish in the top half of the table in twelfth.

Studying the survey in relation to Argyle, our mid-season drop-off in form continued relentlessly for the remainder of the season, and in fact, all the way to Wembley. We lost our way in February/March and despite the odd success here and there, we were completely unable to regain our earlier season form.

Of course, one of the big bonuses for the Argyle fans this season is that we got to go Wembley. We played really well in the play-off semi-finals against Portsmouth, and secured our place in the final with a 91st minute goal in the second leg at Home Park. That game and that goal were the highlights of my season. It was an epic battle with Pompey over two legs, and there is no doubt that we were the better team. As extra time and penalties were looking more and more likely, I was super aware that in football the better team doesn't always win, so when that corner came across and Peter Hartley bundled it into the back of the net, the feeling of utter relief was amazing. Oh my, oh my, the joy of football.

And, on the back of that glorious victory, I got to go and check out a modern top-of-the-range football stadium. Along with 35,000 other Argyle fans and, to be fair, a pretty large number of Wimbledon fans too, we sat in comfort and watched a very, very tense game of football indeed.

Wembley Stadium is amazing. Obviously when the Football Association purchased it, they ticked all the top spec boxes for every item in the online catalogue of stadiums. Walking up Wembley Way with all the fans was so exciting. And entering the stadium and going up the elevators, and walking on the marble floors, and buying a cup of tea without queuing for it, and taking our seats to watch Argyle play in the greatest football stadium in the UK, it was all just great.

Except we bloody lost.

I get back home from the play-off final late the next day. I need a bit of time to relax after the long drive home so I go for a mooch about in the shed. I want to find a few new tools to put out on the stall on Friday, so I start picking through some of the boxes that I have put aside for John to sell at car boot sales.

When I first started my business I used to sell anything that I thought still had some useful life left in it, but over the years I have tried to move the stock upmarket. I have visions of dealing in high value, collectable tools — you know, more money for less work — and I guess if I'm honest, I do like people coming along and seeing the stall and saying, "Hey, Tom, you're getting some nice tools on your stall these days." In reality, I think I made more money when I was more of a tool-recycling centre, but I'm not planning on going back that way.

I manage to put together a small collection of stuff good enough to sell. I am just taking it to my bench ready to clean up in the morning when in comes Alex. I've been waiting for this moment and I know he is going to want to know all about my Wembley trip.

"Hi, Tom. How did it all go mate? Shame about the result."

"Oh hi, Alex. How are you today? Yeah, shame about losing, but hey, I had a great time thanks."

"Yeah, I watched it on Sky. Got to say it wasn't the greatest match ever, was it?"

"No mate, it really wasn't. It was like Argyle never really got going. For some reason we seemed to be a bit scared."

"Yeah, that's what I saw too, Tom," says Alex. "It's a recognised thing that is, it's called the fear factor of failure."

"That sounds about right, but I reckon you might actually mean the fear of failure factor," I reply.

"Yes, it's all about psychology isn't it?" Alex goes on. "I've got this theory."

"Really mate, you do surprise me," I say. We are both laughing now.

"Yes, you know, at that level, in football, the teams have roughly the same levels of skill, and roughly the same levels of fitness, and really, the main difference now is the psychology. You have to get the psychology right. And that is the job of the manager: to get that right in his players. And it looked to me if that was what was wrong with Argyle. They were scared of screwing up and it cost them the game."

"Sounds about right to me," I say.

"Yes, but there's so much more work to be done in this area. Not only have you got to get the team psychology right, you have to work on the individual psychology of each player too. They have to develop psychological stamina. They have to be able to move on when they get things wrong. They have to stay focussed in moments of high drama, and stay focussed after those moments too. The thing is, it is a huge area of the game where improvements can still be made."

"I'm completely with you on all this Alex," I say. "But surely now, most sports at a professional level are onto this aren't they? Liverpool definitely have their resident psychologist and I think England maybe use the same guy."

"Oh yes, for sure, it's happening at the very top of the game. And I'll tell you what, and this is interesting in relation to the play-off final, if you look at the way Liverpool play, admittedly it's a bit erratic at the moment, but when they play well, they really go for it, they take the risks hoping to get the breaks."

"Yes, and quite often it blows up in their face too, doesn't it?" I replied. "It is a very complicated situation isn't it? Because a few times I've watched Liverpool really go for it, and then go behind because of that, and then have to chase the game, and slightly lose heart coming up against a massed defence, and then just end up watching the time run out. And that has to be the least enjoyable spectator experience ever doesn't it?"

"Well yes, if you're on the losing side it does anyway," Alex agrees.

I can see that this conversation could run and run. I don't really mind though because, as usual, it is a subject that I am really interested in. What are the ingredients that go together to make a successful football team? Clearly that is what every club is searching for, but some are searching in a more organised way than others.

And then Alex is off on one again. "The thing is Tom, if you think about using psychology in football, you could say, well, all you need is Sir Alex using his hairdryer in the dressing room. I mean that worked pretty well didn't it?"

"Ah yes, it did, and it's probably a lot easier to get a good manager who can motivate his players, than it is to work on each individual player to motivate themselves, isn't it?" I reply. "But you know what? If you've got Kloppy in the dressing room, he's pretty psyched up, and then you've got a bunch of players that are all individually correctly psyched up too, that's got to be a recipe for success,"

I laugh at the absurdity of it all. "I'll tell you what, I'm not about to go out there and stick a tenner on Liverpool to win the Premier League next season, as much as I'd like them to. But I absolutely do think that if you can put a psychologically well-educated team out there on the pitch, with a clear psychological game plan, you surely must be at a bit of an advantage, mustn't you?"

"Indeed you must," says Alex. "I mean, look at the second half of the Seville game. Seville came out like a bunch of demons, got an early goal, and just absolutely went for it. Liverpool didn't know what was happening. And I bet you Kloppy had psyched them right up too, but they lost it all in 90 seconds."

"God, don't you just love football," I say, and on that note we both fall silent for a moment or two.

"Do you know what, Alex? I hope we keep our manager next season, because I reckon he will see what's happened to Argyle this season and put most of that right. I'd say, get a few quid on Argyle for automatic promotion next season and make a tidy little profit. Got to be a dead cert."

"Well, Tom, I'll probably pass on your betting tips mate, but I'll tell you what though, you know I said I was going to test how luck got on in Super 6? Well, I did it."

"No way Alex, I don't believe you did that. I thought we were discussing that as a joke."

"No, I was serious mate, I worked out the scores like we discussed. I made the spinners, and I entered my results for the last 10 weeks of the season. I admit I did it retrospectively though. I finally worked out my results last night."

"Oh yeah, and how did Lucky Spinner get on then? I bet he did better than I did over the last 10 weeks."

"Well, surprisingly, he didn't do that well. I was

really surprised. He turned in an average score of 4.8, so that's even worse than me."

"Oh my, that's quite heartening isn't it?" I reply. "So a little bit of football knowledge is actually beneficial then. Thanks to you Alex, we finally have definitive proof at last."

"Yes, proof of that alone is well worth the weeks of hard work I put in there making those spinners, wouldn't you agree?" Alex says.

Indeed I would, and you know what? After my blistering start to Super 6 things went rapidly downhill. In fact, my Super 6 season pretty much mirrored Argyle's season perfectly. Up until Barnet away, I was averaging more than nine points a week, but in the last ten weeks of the season I averaged just 5.8. In one week I actually got one big fat zero too. And then in the last-but-one week of the competition, for some reason Argyle's last League game was included in the six. I picked up two points for a correct result there, but we won the game 5-0. Who would ever have predicted that score for God's sake?

"Interesting, isn't it?" says Alex, and as I see he is about to launch into yet another football-related conversation I manage to get in before him.

"Alex, for God's sake sod off and let me finish sorting out my tools," I reply, laughing.

As Alex walks off down the field I can't resist one last comment myself. I rush out of the shed and shout, "Hey Alex, are you going to come and watch Argyle with me next season?" Alex looks around and makes a hand gesture that I unfortunately, or maybe fortunately, can't quite make out.

PART THREE

THERE'S ONLY ONE JOHN BISHOP...

It's halfway through October; we're 12 games into the new season. After losing the first two games we have gone on a 10-match unbeaten run and are now five points clear at the top of the league. Could this be our year?

15TH OCTOBER 2016, PORTSMOUTH (H)

Today I am off to Home Park to watch us play Portsmouth, it's a big game, hyped up as the Dockyard Derby. I am trying to stay calm and not think about it too much. Portsmouth began the season as favourites to win the League, and are now second favourites below Doncaster. We are currently third favourites. Last season in the League, Portsmouth won against us home and away but, crucially, in the play-off semi-final we drew with them at Fratton Park and won the second leg at Home Park. I say the play-off results were crucial, but actually had we taken points off them in the League we may not have ended up in the play-offs anyway, so I'll rephrase that: crucially, we lost both our League games against Portsmouth last season.

A few things have changed for me this season. The crowd at Argyle has steadily increased, and I'm not sure if it's that, or maybe I'm arriving a bit later, but I've lost my regular parking spot in Burleigh Park Road.

At the moment I am driving around and grabbing a spot wherever I can, which I'm not that keen on. I'm thinking I might have to find a regular spot further away and do a longer walk. Another big change is that I have sort of permanently moved out of what used to be the old Lyndhurst, over into the few rows of seats below the Mayflower. There are some big advantages. I like the slightly more sedate atmosphere there — it's mostly old folk — and I absolutely love the refreshment set-up. There is a little window between our seats and what used to be the family enclosure, and in there is a girl selling all the same stuff you can get at all the other outlets, but without the queue. There's just never a big queue, even at half time it is a joy.

I've been thinking quite a bit about the relationship between what you want to get from going to football and where you choose to sit. A simple example would be when we turned up at Barnet last season and made our way to our seats: we were about 30 yards away from what you might call our main vocal support, the Green Army. Josh's partner Rose, who was at her first-ever football match, instantly said, "I want to be over there," whereas my response was, "I need to be a little higher up and a little further back". So nowadays, when I arrive at Home Park, I aim to sit above the tunnel, just slightly towards the Devonport End. Being just above the dugouts is really good too, I get to see a whole load of extra drama going on between the managers and the fourth official. Yes, I'm really growing to like this spot. As someone said the other day, "Where are we all going to go when they redevelop the Mayflower?"

I make my way to the ground and buy my 50/50 tickets. Then I go through the old turnstiles into the undeveloped area of the ground. As soon as I am in there, my mind wanders back to times past and I imagine what it would have been like back in the 1950s and 1960s. At that time the stand would have been almost new, a proud addition to Home Park. I am very familiar with the old photos of crowds of football supporters all wearing flat caps, and the odd youngster with a scarf and rattle. I imagine a large proportion of the crowd would have been dockyard workers in those days too. Things have changed so much since then. Nowadays there are a lot more women at the games and, dare I say it, watching football is not just a hobby of the working class anymore.

I'm even wondering if the fans are bigger now too. Certainly the old seats in our section of the ground are a lot smaller than the seats in the new areas. At the last home game against Yeovil, when I got to my seat it was barely visible, so I decided to sit on some steps nearby. It was actually a great spot and I was feeling pretty pleased with myself, until about 15 minutes into the game when I saw a steward making his way along the stand towards me. He told me that I'd been picked up on CCTV and that he'd received a message through his earpiece to tell me to move. A nearby fan beckoned me over and I ended up with a pretty decent seat anyway. Really I should have bought a season ticket and then I wouldn't have all this uncertainty at the beginning of every game. I wasn't quite sure how many games I would be able to get to this year so I held back, and now I'm paying the price.

When the Lyndhurst Stand was redeveloped in 2001 (completed in 2002), the club sold off the old seats for £5 each. Josh bought one. I remember picking it up and thinking, "This bloody thing is going to be in my shed for the next 50 years". Sure enough, it's still there. When he bought a house a few years ago I tried to unload it on him but he refused to take it, using the excuse that it wouldn't go down well with his partner. I've had a good look on eBay for these seats but to date I haven't been able to find one.

There's something about progress, it doesn't come for free and yes, you gain something, but you always lose something too. When they knock down the Mayflower Stand, well, that's it, it's gone. That piece of history will never ever be experienced again. OK, we'll have the videos (on our smartphones, at least until we upgrade them and then, unless you're smart too, that'll be them gone), but we won't have the experience of watching football at Home Park in the way that people have watched it there for the last 65 years. It will be gone. And then there are the old gents toilets, again a magnificent piece of history. Has anyone, anywhere, preserved an example of some toilets like that, or doesn't it really matter? Maybe I am happy to let them go, I genuinely can't make up my mind on that one. And surely to God, they will keep those old turnstiles? Please tell me no one would ever dream of knocking them down. That last point I am serious about! You know what I would do? I would preserve just that little area, the turnstiles, the toilets, plus a tiny little section of the Mayflower. They could put it on the right as you go into the ground as a tribute to a piece of recent history that will soon be gone forever.

Portsmouth football club have had a pretty torrid time of it over the last few years, both financially and on the football field. Only seven years ago they were in the Premier League. Four years later they were in serious danger of being relegated to the Conference. In 2013 the club was taken over by the Pompey Supporters Trust and thankfully some stability has returned. This season so far, the average attendance at Fratton Park is well over 16,000. They began the season as favourites to win the League but have slipped to second favourites. Doncaster, managed by Darren Ferguson, are the current favourites. The average attendance at Home Park this season is more than 8,000. We began the season as fifth favourites and we are currently third favourites to win the League. However you look at this game today, there is no escaping the fact that it is a huge fixture, and I am nervous.

***

I'm on my way home, driving across the moor towards Princetown. I have to say, getting out of that game with a point was a victory as far as I am concerned. Portsmouth are a good side and a draw was a fair result. We are still top of the League and our unbeaten run continues. When we went 2-1 down with four minutes to go, I couldn't help wondering what was going through Derek Adams's mind. Certainly, I thought the game was lost at that point and that our unbeaten run was over. I didn't expect to win today anyway, I didn't really expect to draw; I was expecting to lose. I was anticipating feeling some relief from the loss because, to be frank, the pressure of this unbeaten run is beginning to get to me. What the pressure must have been like when the manager did his 40-match unbeaten run at Ross County I can't imagine. And that run ended with a goal five minutes from the end, too. What on earth did that feel like when it was all over? But, amazingly, we equalised with an unbelievable strike from Connor Smith in the 89th minute, and the run continues. God I love football (sometimes)!

On Radio 5 is a commentary of the Palace v West Ham game so I switch over to Radio Devon, just in time to catch the Derek Adams post-match interview. Both he and the presenter were going on about the bias of the officials in relation to the three yellow cards handed out to Argyle players, although I have to say I didn't notice this myself. Adams was saying it is well known that Paul Cook, the Portsmouth manager, seeks to gain advantage by getting at the officials. I've watched Cook. He is a lively manager, and he does have a go. It was quite something to watch when he went head to head with Adams in the play-off semi-final last season. I admire these guys for their passion, and of course for their skill and knowledge. Both these managers have put together really good teams and, hats off to both of them, that was one of the best games at Home Park this season so far. Hopefully we'll be playing against Portsmouth next season too.

***

It's early Sunday morning and I have finally managed to find some time to get out in the shed and take a closer look at something I picked up at the market on Friday. My friend Darren, who mainly deals in door furniture and old brass fittings, quite often collects a bunch of old tools for me to have a look at. And this time, right in the middle of them was this really old beaten-up brass and steel clamp. As soon as I saw it I wanted it. I had no idea what it was but I just had this feeling that it was a bit special. It turns out that it is a swan shot gang mould, a tool for making lead shot for firing from a musket.

It's not in good condition. It has one handle missing and the other one is a modern file handle that has just been rammed on to the old tang. It is well battered and it doesn't open properly to allow the user to remove the newly made shot. But it is going to look great by the time I get it fixed up. Finding interesting old stuff is the best part of my job, I love it, and I am really quite excited about this shot mould. There's not much I can do with it right now though. I need to find some authentic-looking handles and work out what's wrong with the hinge that is stopping it from opening.

I am just putting it up on my 'precious item' shelf when there is a knock on the door, and in walks Alex. "Hi, Tom, how are you this morning?"

"Oh hi, Alex, why are you about so bright and early?"

"I had one of those nights Tom. I've got so much to do and I really needed a good sleep, but I couldn't sleep for worrying about everything I had to do, so annoying."

"Oh yeah," I reply, "I get that too, and then when I get up I'm so tired all I want to do is go back to bed, and then I'm tired all day and then I get cross, and so it goes on."

"Still never mind, how's the big weekend going so far for you?" Alex asks.

"Well, I was more than relieved to come away with a point against Portsmouth. They are a strong outfit and to be honest we were up against it for a lot of the match. And I'll tell you what, mate, I'll be more than happy if Liverpool come away with a point against Man U tonight."

"Oh come on," says Alex, "we're going to win easily tonight. Man U have been poor so far this season."

"Yes, the important words in that sentence, Alex, are 'so far'. This is the ideal match for them to win and turn their season around. Don't get too cocky. I'll tell you what, Alex, I don't know if it's just me getting more involved in this football malarkey, or if something is really changing here. The whole football scene seems to be getting so much more intense these days."

"Yes, you're right, Tom, it is all very pressurised right now."

There is a short silence as we have a little think about things, and then an explanation comes. "The thing is this, Tom, you're feeling the pressure at Argyle because you are top of the League. You were top or thereabouts at this point last year too and then you blew it, so you are bound to be nervous about that one. And then, on top of that, you have the pressure of the unbeaten run, which is ridiculous really. To be honest, you're probably making more of that right now than Derek Adams is."

"Yes, he's probably going, 'Och, it's just one game at a time'," I say in my disastrous attempt at a Scottish accent. "And then of course there is the Liverpool situation. Suddenly, after years and years, it is beginning to look like we have got a real chance of being a top team again. But we are all on the edge of our seats because we have got used to the years and years of inconsistency. The whole situation just seems to get more and more fascinating."

"You won't believe this though," says Alex, "I had it all planned out to watch the match at the Union, and then I realised that today is Sam's birthday so I'm thinking going to the football might not be the best way forward."

"Take her with you mate. Tell her it's her birthday treat, She'll love it," I laugh.

"Yeah, right," laughs Alex as he walks out of the shed.

There is something about Manchester United that intrigues me. Well, there is lots about them that intrigues me, but this one particular thing really, really intrigues me. Why do I hate them? Like so many people of my age, my introduction to the world of football was on the morning of 6th February 1958. We woke up to the news of the Munich plane crash. I was seven years old and that was the day I became seriously aware of the world of professional football. Three months later Man U beat Fulham 5-3 in the FA Cup semi-final replay. The 1958 Cup Final, between Man U and Bolton Wanderers, was the first game that we watched on our very first, newly purchased, black-and-white television. Man U lost 2-0 and Nat Lofthouse controversially bundled Harry Gregg into the net for the second goal. Harry Gregg was one of the four survivors of the Munich air crash playing in that game. The emotions were a little full on in our house that day. It was all a bit too much for a seven-year-old boy to deal with.

Interestingly, at that point I was a Manchester United supporter. So what happened along the way? Well, my next overpowering memory of Man U was in 1963 when they again reached the Cup Final. They were up against Leicester City, who had finished fourth in the League. Man U had finished 19th and on top of that they had lost both of their League games against Leicester. To me it seemed like a formality that Leicester would win. In fact, I was so convinced of this that I bet my entire week's pocket money on a Leicester victory. The boy that I had the bet with was Richard Clarke — we didn't really get on. I don't remember why, but one day he had decided that I needed to be beaten up and he had twisted my neck so hard it made me cry. I needed revenge and Leicester were my big hope.

As they say, the rest is history. Manchester United won the game in the 85th minute, and I then had to undergo the excruciating experience of handing over to my nemesis what in those days we still called two shillings. Looking back, I'd say the events of that day were most probably the seeds of what then went on to become an intense dislike of Man U. For years, every weekend I have had this thing where I have nine points I can win: I win three if Argyle win, three if Liverpool win, and three more if Man U lose. As you can imagine, over the last 30 years I've rarely scored nine points and more often than not I've scored three or less. Of course, things have picked up since Fergie retired, and then Derek Adams pitched up, and then Liverpool got Kloppy. I've had a few nines in recent years, but all a little too late really, because as it turns out my hatred for the Reds has begun to mellow over the last few years too.

It makes me wonder if somehow Fergie was to blame for causing such a negative reaction in me, and so many other people, towards that great club. Maybe I couldn't stomach all the winning that went on there for 20 years or so. Somehow I picked up the feeling that they were being a bit smug about things too. And then you'd hear Alan Green say things like he couldn't understand why English football fans wanted Manchester United to lose against European opposition, and I'd be thinking, sorry mate, I happen to understand that perfectly well.

As it turns out, in the end I quite liked Fergie. I liked the way he stood up for the ordinary people and he was clearly a brilliant manager. Since then of course, it's been all downhill for Manchester United. David Moyes had a terrible time, and then came LVG, what a disaster. And then, beyond any non-Man U fan's wildest dreams, they appointed Mourinho, who you'd have to say is about as un-Man U as you could get. Mind you, if he starts winning a few things that will definitely put the cat amongst the pigeons.

Anyway, whichever way you slice it, this evening's game is a six-pointer. Argyle won me one point on Saturday, so I am destined for a total of one or seven. What happens if it's a draw tonight? Well, that will be one point for Liverpool and one for Man U, so I will get none, but I'd still take a draw for sure.

Contrary to Alex's remark that Derek Adams is probably not concerned about the 11-match unbeaten run, he clearly is. In his interview on the Plymouth Player HD app, when asked about the importance of the last-minute equaliser against Portsmouth, he actually mentioned that the draw keeps the run going. It looks to me as if he is using the run as a motivating force, and it seems to be working.

I'm formulating a plan to entice Alex to come and watch Argyle with me. Whenever I'm with him, I slightly get the feeling that he wants me to put the pressure on him a bit to get him to say that he will come to a match with me. Imagining what other people are thinking is something I have a policy of avoiding. It can lead to a lot of very dodgy communications. But in this case I can't see how it can cause any harm, and I quite want him to see the way Argyle are playing at the moment.

I can hear him coming up the yard now. He must need to borrow something or, if I am being more charitable, maybe he just wants a chat.

"Hi, Tom," he calls out when he sees the shed light is on.

"Hi, Alex, how are you mate, how did your birthday night out go?"

"Well," Alex replies, "it was a disaster. Halfway through the meal Sam says, and I quote, 'Alex, it feels like you want to be somewhere else'."

We both laugh at that. I could see that 'the disaster' had been quite serious, but thankfully it looked like they had survived it. "What did you say, Alex? 'Liverpool are on the telly and I'm stuck in this restaurant. Of course I want to be somewhere else'?"

"No, I flat-out denied it and I tried to make a bit more effort to get into the spirit of the evening, but it was pretty clear Sam knew something was wrong. Anyway, she was like a terrier on the way home, she wouldn't leave it alone. In the end she caught me checking the result on my phone and she went absolutely bonkers. Anyway, after she'd had her flip-out she started laughing at the absurdity of it all, and amazingly, in the end we had a nice evening. Thank God."

"Well, that's good then, Alex, and maybe that will teach you to tell the truth, eh? Although I have to say, that was a tricky spot you were in there."

I decide that while we are having a bit of a laugh it might be a good time to start putting my plan into action. "Alex, you know that you never go to watch football?"

"Yeah," he replies, looking a bit nervous.

"Well, how about this for an idea? You know you reckoned the winning run Argyle are on probably didn't matter to the manager? Well, it did because he mentioned it after the match. But what I am going to say is this: Argyle have gone 11 League games without losing. Like last season, I'm going to the away game at Barnet. It is seven games away, on January 2nd. If we are still on our unbeaten run, would you like to come with me?"

"Oooh, I'm not sure about that, Tom. I'll tell you what, I'll have a think and let you know."

"OK mate, you do that," I say. "In the middle of those seven games we play Doncaster too, so it's a bit of a long shot anyway. But I'd love you to take a look at how well Argyle are playing at the moment."

"I'll let you know," Alex repeats as he makes a pretty swift exit. If he did want to borrow something he has clearly forgotten all about it now.

Well, that was a better result than I expected. I'd say from that, that I was definitely right about him wanting me to put a bit of pressure on him to go to a match. But I'm already half regretting what I have just done. I hate inviting people to go to things and then spending the whole time I'm there worrying if they are enjoying it or not. Now I'm imagining me trying to watch the match, sitting next to Alex having a meltdown as his past experiences surge back through his memory. Sometimes I wish I wasn't such a do-gooder. Why the hell does it matter if Alex ever goes to a match again or not?

The Manchester United v Liverpool game was a tense affair. Both teams were desperate not to lose, and Mourinho's tactics — you would have to say his correctly chosen tactics — stifled Liverpool completely. But as I said to Alex earlier, to come away with a point in that game is fine. Sometimes it is not about winning, it is about not losing, and that is part of football. Of course the Press make a big deal out of it, seeing it as shortcomings in the squad, or running out of ideas and so on, but I don't think it is a big deal. If Liverpool win most of their games against the smaller clubs, and win a few of their games against the Big Five, then they are going to be there or thereabouts at the end of the season.

Jurgen Klopp is the best thing to happen at Liverpool for years. He is so 'Liverpool'. The style of football he has the team playing is just so exciting and I look forward to watching every game I possibly can. I know Suarez, Sturridge and Sterling were amazing, and that the 2013/14 season was great, but it bears no comparison to what is happening now. This is not a team built around one great player. This is a great squad put together by a great manager. I have high hopes, which is a rare and dangerous experience for me.

While the 2013/14 season was fantastic, one of the things that really sticks in my mind about it — and indeed the whole time that Brendan Rodgers managed Liverpool — were the post-match interviews (in fact, all of his interviews). It was like listening to a politician. Nothing ever got said, it was almost 100 per cent waffle. Compare that to Jurgen, when he just lets it go. He says what he thinks, and OK, sometimes he spots he has said a bit more than perhaps he should have and he kind of covers things up a bit in the next sentence, but it's all interesting stuff. He doesn't appear to be hiding anything, and if I can be a little bit corny here, he speaks from the heart. It's just so refreshing. It's how the team plays too. Love it, love it, love it!

***

I'd like to be able to tell you that my Super 6 season is going as well as Argyle's and Liverpool's seasons are going right now, but I'm afraid I can't. I've been having a disastrous time and, after 18 weeks, I am averaging just 7.4 points per round. The leaders are averaging around 11.5 which, if it goes anything like last season, will come down to around ten. So for me to make up an average of 2.5 points a week I need to be scoring 12.5. Last week I managed a measly four. How can I be getting it so wrong?

There have been some big developments concerning the spinner, or Lucky Spinner, as he is now named. For the 2016/17 season I have taken over as his operator, and we have formed a league with a total of six members in it. So far, after 18 weeks Lucky has been averaging 4.55 per round, which I would say is pretty conclusive evidence that luck alone will not win you anything at Super 6. I think I have worked out why things aren't going so well for him. Even though he uses the correct ratio of the number of goals scored by each team, which we originally thought would give him the edge over mere humans, the mistake he makes is that he does not take into account what you might call the 'obvious result'. He pays no attention to form, so he might go 4-1 against Arsenal when they are playing Sunderland, of course it could happen, but really it's pretty unlikely.

I decided that I needed to refine him in some way. What I decided to do was give him a bit of common sense. I came up with the idea of using the same spinner results each week, but add one goal to the team which the bookies reckoned were most likely to win. This would change a few results in the direction of what is more likely to happen. My plan was to do this for a few weeks and see if it would improve his average score. I put the idea to the other League members, and to my surprise it was totally rejected. Not one other member of the League wanted Lucky Spinner to change in any way. And that is how Gary Guesstimate was born. We now have a completely new character in the League who has just that tiny bit more football knowledge than Lucky Spinner.

Of course, the story does not end there. Once I had the idea of making modifications to the system, it was no time at all before I felt the need to do more. The obvious thing is to have a character that uses the bookies' predictions and the most common scoreline as their entry to Super 6 each week. Pretty much on the same day that I worked this out, I decided to check out a recent upturn in form by one of the other League members. It turns out that this guy had reached the exact same conclusion and had decided that it was definitely the way to go.

I need to have a chat with Alex about all this Super 6 stuff. I haven't seen him for a few weeks, which is a bit odd because normally he drops by pretty regularly. It is a beautiful morning in early December. A totally clear blue sky and a light frost covering the ground. I walk out to the shed with the vague idea of starting work on a lovely old woodwork vice that I came across the previous week. I have never seen one like it before. It has a very ornate front with the words 'The Twentieth Century – British Made' cast into the moulding. I spent quite a bit of time the night before trying to find information about it online. I did find a few pictures but drew a total blank on any interesting facts about its history. If I get around to it, I'll send some pictures in to a tool collectors forum that I have often used before in my search for information.

I once found a totally unmarked plane that had a really good feel in my hand. I knew that it was a good quality tool, but for selling purposes the maker's name is everything. I put a few pictures up on *lumberjocks.com*, one of my favourite tool nerd sites, and bingo, back came a reply from Don at Time Tested Tools in the USA, who must surely be the world's foremost authority on hand planes. It turns out that my plane was made by the Ohio Tool Company in 1911, and Don also backed me up on the quality factor and explained to me that the heavier design of the blade was one of the reasons that it was such a good plane to use.

A few weeks later at the market, I spotted a young guy holding the plane in his hands and he was sort of imagining standing at his bench using it. I knew that he was feeling that same quality I had felt when I first found it. I wandered over and told him all of the information that Don had given me about the plane. Without any hesitation he asked me if I would be happy to put it under the table while he went to get some cash from the machine. Sometimes I struggle to sell beautiful tools because I just want to keep them. It really does make it much easier to sell them when they find a good home.

I can hear Alex's tractor down the field, so I decide to take a wander down there and see how things are going. The tractor is ticking over nicely, that kind of slow tick over with a nice soft rhythm that you get with old tractors, but I can see no sign of Alex. As I get closer I see him scrabbling about in the hedge.

"Hi, Alex, what are you up to this morning?" I shout out.

"Oh hi, Tom," he replies, "I'm tidying up this hedgerow before I put up a new fence. I don't like leaving all this old wire around the place."

"I haven't seen you for a while. I wondered if you're OK?" I ask.

"Yeah, I'm OK thanks, Tom," he replies, and then that is it, he doesn't say anything else. He just carries on working and I carry on standing there for what seems like quite a while, until I start to feel a little bit odd.

So then I just ask, "What's up, Alex? You're never this quiet. Has something happened?"

"Well, yes it has actually," Alex replies. "I found out

that James told you all about my past. I knew something was going on because of all that bollocks about you trying to get me to go and watch Argyle. I guessed what had happened and when I confronted him he confirmed it."

"Ah, OK," I say, feeling quite uncomfortable now.

"No, not OK," says Alex. "My life is none of your business, and as for all that 'trying to help me' stuff that you got into, I don't need that. I'm fine without you guys, thanks. I know where my life begins and ends, which is clearly more than you and James know about yours."

"Yeah, OK, Alex, you have a point. I'm sorry I overstepped the mark like that." There is another long silence and I decide the best thing to do is to leave.

"Sorry mate, see you later," I say, and walk back up the field. Wow, that isn't the best start to the day. I hate falling out with anyone, and especially with a neighbour. I get back to the shed and decide that I need to lose myself in the world of vintage tools. Time passing sorts out most things in my experience.

***

I'm counting the weeks to Barnet Away. It's less than a month to go now.

19TH NOVEMBER TO 3RD DECEMBER 2016, THE WHEELS COME OFF...

Our winning run came to an end in spectacular style. We lost 3-0 at home to Grimsby. Needless to say, in my totally unbiased and objective opinion, we were clearly the better team that day, they just happened to score three goals and we didn't score any. Worse followed when three days later, in a Tuesday evening fixture, we lost at home again, this time 2-0 against Barnet. And in this game I do admit that we were the second-best team.

Watching Barnet has turned into a bit of a thing for me. Some time ago I read an article about football fans who go to matches not to watch the team or to get caught up in the score or the result, but to watch one player. They watch them for the whole game, whether they have the ball or not. Now, I'm not saying that is what I did, but I was really conscious of the amount of time I spent watching my old favourite, the Barnet centre-forward John Akinde. He is having another good season, currently the top scorer in League Two with 15 goals so far.

Concentrating on watching one player does add another dimension to football. And now I come to think about it, presumably that's what football scouts do, and presumably also, all the top clubs are closely monitoring what all their players are up to whenever they are not in the centre of the action. Akinde is a big guy. He plays as an old-fashioned centre-forward. He is hungry for goals and his finishing is clinical. His other main role appears to be that whenever any defender in his vicinity gets the ball, he hurtles towards them with total menace. During this match it was pretty scary, and there were several occasions when the defender clearly rushed to get rid of the ball rather than risk getting clattered by such a huge bloke. I never saw him run at full tilt for more than about ten yards, and once the ball was gone he quickly reverted to being the big guy hanging about up front. He spends a fair amount of time just standing around.

If I'm honest here, he didn't look that fit to me, but that didn't stop him from being very effective. We didn't really find a way of dealing with him, and yet again he put the ball in the back of our net with a lovely low shot from a through ball. Classic Akinde!

Big centre-forwards are a bit of a problem for us. We came unstuck in the play-off final after Wimbledon brought on Adebayo Akinfenwa as a second-half substitute. Akinfenwa has a bit of a career going on as what you might call 'a phenomenon'. He is massive and in 2014 he was ranked as the strongest footballer in the world. His nickname is 'The Beast', he has his own clothing range called 'Beast Mode On', and he has more than one million followers on his social media sites. When he came on to the field at Wembley, there was a palpable drop in the level of confidence amongst the Argyle fans. His presence definitely contributed to the confusion and panic in our defence that led to Wimbledon's first goal. And then, after a foul in the last minute of the seven minutes of injury time, he grabbed the ball off his team's designated penalty taker and successfully scored to seal the result.

Immediately following the play-off final, The Beast was released by Wimbledon. He promptly made the following announcement on social media: "I think I'm technically unemployed, so any managers, hit me up on WhatsApp." He received a text back from the Wycombe manager, Gareth Ainsworth, and that was it, at the age of 34 he became a Wycombe player. But, and some might say unfortunately, the story doesn't end there. On Boxing Day we play Wycombe at Home Park. To coincide with our dip in form, Wycombe are on a seven-match winning streak that has taken them up to sixth in the table. I remember back to watching the same fixture last year. It was not an enjoyable experience. Wycombe Wanderers are a desperate outfit.

So here we are in the middle of December, and that oh so familiar anxious feeling is back. The following Saturday we lose again, this time to Morecambe who are struggling down in 20th place. What on earth is going on? In the space of one week, our 14-match unbeaten run has turned into a three-match losing run. I text Josh and Henry to remind them to keep the Play-off Final day clear in their diaries. In a week's time we play Newport at home in the Cup. They are bottom of the League, so surely this will be the turning point and we can get on our way again.

Can you believe it, we don't even win against Newport. We draw 0-0 at home. Why is Roy of the Rovers nowhere to be seen when you need him most?

I look back to all the sandcastles in the sky that I have constructed in my life, and how, as I get older, I have watched these sandcastles dissolve in front of my very eyes. I have sandcastles that I have unknowingly constructed in my landscape that I can't even see. Sandcastles that I don't even know exist until they begin to fall apart. As time goes by, the reality dawns: maybe there is not a lot of this stuff that actually matters that much in the end.

I have clung on to some ideas for years and years, only to think later on, actually, where is the reality in that? And among all this, the world appears to become ever more crazy, which is actually the opposite to what I thought was going to happen (yes, another of my sandcastles). So where is the sense in all this? What is real and what is really, truly worth hanging on to? Or, to put it more simply, which are the bits I like the best?

There is a knock at the door of the shed and in walks Alex. "Hi, mate," I say.

"Hi, Tom, sorry about earlier, mate. I really should have handled that better than I did."

"No worries, Alex. Life goes on," I reply. "Are you OK now?"

"Yeah, I'm fine, Tom. I'm just a bit over-sensitive about all that football crap, but if you're happy to forget it so am I."

"Yep, Alex, I already have," I laugh. "In the end not too much matters, does it mate? I always think of the Bill Shankly quote, how does it go? You know the one: 'Some people believe football is a matter of life and death. I can assure you it is much, much more important than that'."

"Yes, that's the trouble isn't it?" says Alex. "Football becomes everything. That's exactly what happened to me when I was a kid, and that's why I hit the skids in the way that I did. I made a mistake. When I was told to pack my bags, I shouldn't have gone on a bender, I should have calmly looked for another club and carried on. Who knows how it would have turned out."

"Alex, that kind of talk will drive you crazy. Of course we all think like that. I wonder how many really big 'what if' questions each person has in their lives. I once had an idea for a book where in each big 'what if' moment in my life, I took the other choice to the one that I actually took. I wrote a few pages, it was fun. It was like living the life I could have lived. But of course it was all total fiction, because anything could have happened. I mean, that beautiful girl you walked away from, she could actually have been a total nightmare. Chances are she was too, mate. Just don't get into the what ifs mate, not with any seriousness anyway."

"Yes, Tom, I know you're right. Most of the time I am fine, but all this football chat, and then you getting on my case like that, I just blew a fuse. But hey, on a brighter note, have you seen what John's been up to in our Super 6 League?"

"Yeah, interesting isn't it? His 2-1 predictions on the bookies' favourites technique hasn't passed me by, if that's what you mean."

"Yeah, that's exactly what I mean," says Alex. He then goes on to tell me about a situation one of his mates found himself in a few years ago. He was in a Super 6 league with all the guys at his work, and there was this one guy who had no interest in football and he wouldn't join in. Anyway, they kept hassling him and eventually he agreed to play. He turned out to be really good at it and it wasn't long before he was topping the League. After a while they worked out what he was up to. Every week he was going down the bookies, checking the odds and sticking on the old faithful 2-1 with the favourite to win, in every match.

So what's the deal for everyone else when someone starts operating that system? It's a difficult situation, because if it truly does work it kind of makes the game a bit of a non-starter. The thing is, there are two parts to Super 6. There is the prize for the whole season, and then there is the weekly prize. So by doing the 2-1 stunt you are pretty much saying that you are not going for the weekly prize. I mean, what are the chances of six 2-1s coming up? But you are in with a big chance of the overall season prize because you are using the best football brains in the world — the bookies' odds — combined with the most likely scoreline. In the end, Alex's mate and his friends asked the guy not to play anymore because it was spoiling their fun. Yes indeed, it's all very interesting.

I spend a while pondering the future of Super 6. And then I realise that it is an easy thing to check out if the 2-1 system actually is the spoiler that it appears

to be. I go to the leaderboard for the season so far and
check this week's results for what is called the Global
Top 15. Phew, not one of them is doing the 2-1. The
first thing I realise is that by going with the bookies'
prediction you automatically take out the draw as a
selection. The bookies never make the draw the favourite
over a win. The top 15 players predicted a draw in
just under two out of the six games. And then I count
up the 2-1 predictions and they average out at just
under two per player. And then the final proof that
the 2-1 system is not the holy grail it appears to be:
the top 15 players averaged 14.3 points each in that
one week. That is a phenomenal average considering
that the overall leader in Week 21 has a total of 244
points, which is an average of 11.6 per round.

Plymouth Argyle haven't played against Liverpool for 54 years.
The last time we played them was at Home Park in April 1962
in the old Division Two. We lost 3-2. That season, Liverpool,
managed by Bill Shankly, won promotion to Division One.
They have been in the top flight of English football ever since.
In 1962 I was 11 years old, and I didn't really have a favourite
football team. I had never seen Liverpool play, and I only knew
of Plymouth Argyle because of their name being read out on
Sports Report at five o'clock every Saturday afternoon.

On the Monday evening, two days after we scramble a
draw against Newport in the FA Cup, the news comes
up on my phone that the winner of the replay will be
playing Liverpool at Anfield. Suddenly my feelings
about the result of that replay go from "I don't really

care" to "Oh my God, we really do have to win that game!". I start to imagine what it will be like to visit Anfield, and to watch my two favourite teams playing against each other. Obviously I will be supporting Plymouth Argyle, and obviously we haven't got a chance of winning, and obviously I don't care anyway. I just want to go to Anfield, and watch Liverpool, and see Kloppy, and if we get away with anything under about 5-0 I will call that a result.

We win the replay against Newport 1-0, with Graham Carey scoring a penalty in the 113th minute. Can you believe it? We're all off to Anfield, and I get my first chance to visit a Premier League ground, and my first chance to watch Liverpool for real or, should I say, not on the telly.

The last 18 months or so have been an interesting time for me as a football fan. For years I have watched Argyle and mourned the fact that they would never be like Liverpool. And then Derek Adams comes along, and of course we're not like Liverpool, but everyone can see that we are really trying to be a good footballing side. In the replay against Newport, at one point the commentator actually said, and I quote, "Argyle are doing some high pressing here". I couldn't believe he'd said it. And then, after going into the lead against Wycombe the other day, a chant broke out around the ground which really said it all for me. Maybe it's not original but I've never heard it before:

> *2-1 to the football team,*
> *2-1 to the football team,*
> *2-1 to the football team.*

Much laughter and such a good feeling, and long may Home Park be blessed with good football.

2ND JANUARY 2017, BARNET (A)

One week to go until Barnet away. A lot can change over nine months. I remember the chaos I got into with my travel arrangements for the last trip to Barnet. This time I am super confident about the whole thing. I've bought my train ticket online and this year I don't need a printout to pick it up at the station. I have a six-figure code to punch into the ticket machine. I also now know how to use my debit card on The Tube instead of buying a ticket. So what could possibly go wrong?

Five weeks ago, a few days after Barnet had beaten Argyle at Home Park, Martin Allen handed in his resignation to become the new manager of the National League club Eastleigh FC. Rossi Eames, the Barnet youth team coach, was named as the new 'interim' Barnet manager.

Martin Allen replaced Ronnie Moore, who had been at Eastleigh for three months. Ronnie Moore is now rumoured to be the likely replacement for Kenny Jackett, who recently resigned at Rotherham after 39 days. Kenny Jackett is hotly tipped to be the next manager at Barnet FC. The only problem is that Rossi Eames is doing rather well as the interim manager, having won two out of his four games in charge.

The three o'clock kick off gives me plenty of time to travel up to Barnet in the morning, have some lunch and get to the ground for the match. As I pull into the half-empty car park at Exeter station, I am quietly confident of my routine. I park the van so that I can easily see the number plate from the ticket machine. The first thing I notice is that the price of parking has gone up yet again. These guys really do know how to make money. Luckily I have plenty of coins so I punch in my registration number, put in the pile of coins and take my ticket. I get back to the van and check the ticket to make sure all is well, only to see that I have just paid £9.40 for three hours' of car parking. How the hell has that happened? I go back to the machine and after some time I see that £9.40 is the daily fee if you book over the phone. On a sign well above my eye line is a sign saying that if you pay cash at the machine the fee is £10.40. Needless to say there is no way to add an extra pound to correct my mistake.

Looking back now I think I should have just put the ticket in the van window and maybe put a note explaining what had happened, but I don't do that. I humbly go into the station, buy myself a coffee and spend a very unrestful 20 minutes on the phone to Apcoa car parks, trying to find a human being to speak to, which I completely fail to do. I end up buying a 24-hour ticket for another £9.40. Altogether an inauspicious, and expensive, start to the day, and here's hoping things can only get better.

I meet up with Josh at King's Cross as planned, and we arrive at The Hive a good hour before kick off. I had bought the tickets for the match off the Argyle website and we had to pick them up from the ticket office. I pass the printout of my receipt to the guy and he goes over to a well organised box of tickets all neatly stacked in envelopes in alphabetical order. I watch as he goes twice through the Ws. Needless to say, our tickets aren't there. He makes his way back to the window and explains that because we are Argyle fans we have to go around to the away end and there will be a temporary ticket office around there where we can pick up our tickets.

When we get to the away end there is no sign of a ticket office and the stewards send us back to where we have just come from. All a bit predictable really. This time things are slightly different though. By now there are about a dozen Argyle fans who have all been on the same journey, brandishing their receipts and demanding their tickets. Stopping us from getting our tickets is a guy dressed in a fancy suit, obviously someone high up on the admin staff at the club. The problem is that our receipts don't have barcodes and he is worried that we have all been printing out endless copies so that our mates can get in for free. He holds his ground for a while, but as the pressure inevitably builds up he finally realises he has nowhere to go and gives way. The tickets are printed out and we are in.

***

Barnet away round two is, in lots of ways, pretty similar to Barnet away round one. We start off in a bit of a muddle and never really manage to settle down. Our old adversary John Akinde, scorer of 17 goals so far this season, doesn't really cause us any problems in his own right, but the attention his very presence demands leaves open the opportunity for Mauro Vilhete to bang in a goal from a shortish corner in the 14th minute. As ever, I begin to look for the benefits in our situation. Going ahead early in a game isn't always the best thing. Suddenly Barnet have something to protect and something to lose. Admittedly we now need to score a goal but we have so much time, and we are a good team. We play good football, and we have Graham Carey, and our manager is really good and, and, and... Surely in over an hour and a quarter we are going to score a goal, but we don't. We lose 1-0 at Barnet for the second time in nine months.

I come away from the match feeling fine. I actually enjoyed it. What is happening to me? Why doesn't it matter to me if we win or lose anymore? Is it just that I am getting old?

And then I get my answer. Josh turns and asks me if I enjoyed the game and I say straight out without thinking, "Yes, I loved it, but do you know what, if Argyle ever give up trying to play good football I wouldn't go and see them anymore. That would be it for me. I am an Argyle fan for sure, but above that I am a fan of good football. I am a fan of the Beautiful Game. Right now this is the most I have ever enjoyed watching Plymouth Argyle and long may it remain this way."

We walk away from The Hive through the almost-familiar car park and up onto Camrose Avenue. It is a bitterly cold day and my feet are freezing. Not enough to make me cry, but enough for me to wish that I'd put on an extra pair of socks that morning. I watch on my screen as the Uber slowly makes its way towards us. Getting into a nice warm Toyota Prius and chatting to the driver about Uber or Bangladesh, in this moment this is my idea of heaven.

8TH JANUARY 2017, LIVERPOOL (A)

So that is where this little book is supposed to end, but I can't just
leave it here. When I planned the book I didn't factor in one small
thing. I did not foresee that we would be drawn to play Liverpool
at Anfield in the third round of the FA Cup. My two teams playing
against each other, and both of them possibly playing the best
football they have played for years. I am first and foremost an
Argyle supporter now, but I will always love Liverpool FC. I am
so excited to be going to Anfield, and so excited to maybe see
some of the great players that I have only ever watched on the
telly. I know Kloppy will play his youngsters, it's the right thing to
do. It's what he did against Exeter last year when Exeter managed
to get a draw at St James Park.

Obviously we're not going to win. We're probably going to
lose about 4-0 and I don't mind if we do. The only thing is, if we
could possibly hold the tide back for long enough we might get
to see Adam Lallana, or Roberto Firmino, or Daniel Sturridge
come off the bench. God I'd love that!

Do you ever get that thing where you admire someone who is
really good at something and automatically imagine that they are
a good bloke? I get it a lot, it happens to me with rock stars and
actors and TV personalities, and of course it happens to me with
footballers too. You kind of idolise the person and imagine that
to be that good at something you must also be a good bloke, and
then the next thing you know there is that very same bloke all over
the media because they have made some awful racist comment,
or some really derogatory remarks about women, or even worse
got involved in not very nice stuff at all.

I've slightly got a few heroes myself at the moment. I'm desperately
trying not to have, because I know we are all only human, and in
the end we are all equal. We all live in the duality of this world
and we all face the same dilemmas. I know the appearance of the

dilemmas may differ, but the nature of them is the same. Anyway, back to the heroes. I am 66 years old and I have a favourite footballer, what an admission! He doesn't play for Argyle, he plays for Liverpool and I always imagine he is a good bloke. He might be a nightmare for all I know. Another person I slightly hero worship at the moment is Derek Adams. Is he a good bloke? I have no idea. And what about Kloppy? I mean, you don't get to the top of the management game, or any part of football for that matter, unless you are ruthless and majorly competitive. Neither of those qualities is necessarily a particularly nice character trait.

Kloppy is an interesting guy. He seems to have found a way to combine all the qualities needed to be a successful manager and a successful human being at the same time. By the way, in case it's not clear, I don't really buy into the meaning of 'success' as pedalled by the powers that be in this society. I'm calling a successful human being one who understands that respect and kindness towards other people is more important than their own ambition.

It's two days before the Liverpool match. I'm back from doing the market and I decide to empty my van before I quit for the day. Just as I am finishing up I hear the familiar sound of James's old Land Rover making its way up the hill towards the shed. He sees that I am about and stops by for a chat.

"Hi, Tom."

"Oh hi, James, how are you doing today?"

"Good, Tom, thanks. Sorry about what happened the other day, mate."

"Oh right, you mean that little fall-out I had with Alex? Yeah that was a bit difficult for a while there. But we've sorted it out OK, I think," I reply.

"Yeah, that was my fault, Tom, I never should have told you all that stuff that I know about Alex's illustrious past. I just never imagined that it would all blow up in our faces like that."

"Not to worry. You just didn't factor in my over-zealous do-gooder mentality, mate. It's bugged me all my life. One day I will rein it in, I hope."

"Are you off to Liverpool this weekend then?" asks James.

"Certainly am," I reply. "I'll tell you what, James, my mate Ken, he's a season-ticket holder at Argyle. He gave me his ticket if you fancy going. you'll be sitting on your own though, not anywhere near to where we'll be."

"Ah no, I can't make it this weekend, I've got to look after the kids while my missus has a break. Why don't you offer it to Alex?" He laughs. "He's a Liverpool supporter."

I am laughing at the absurdity of the situation now. "It does seem a shame doesn't it? I mean, he's always banging on about Lallana this and Firmino that. He would absolutely love it."

"I'll tell you what, Tom, leave the ticket in the shed, maybe on that red vice, and I'll drop it into the conversation that it's there. I'll tell him that you are leaving it for me but I can't use it."

"Cool idea, James. I'll do that then. Don't make it too obvious will you?"

"Of course not, Tom, he won't suspect a thing. I'd better crack on, mate, loads to do this evening."

"OK, mate, catch you later then, bye."

***

We arrive at Liverpool Lime Street station and get a taxi up to the ground. There we meet up with Henry, who has driven up from Wales. This is the second time in a year that the four of us have been to a match together, the last one being the play-off final. I can't actually remember the last time that Sarah went to a match before that. This feels just like the old days, except of course that we are at Anfield and are all wildly over-excited.

It is a couple of hours before kick off and we are with some friends who regularly visit Anfield to support Liverpool. The first stop is Homebaked, the community-owned bakery just over the road from the stadium, where we buy pies for lunch. The menu includes, amongst other things, Shankley Pie and Scouse Pie, plus a couple of veggie options, including a mushroom pie, which I choose. It is absolutely delicious. Just in case this is as close as I get to being a food reviewer, I will make a bit more effort on the description of the pie: the pastry is great and so is the filling. And by the way, the ambience of the place is just what you would expect in Liverpool, really friendly and welcoming. Let's put it this way, I'll definitely be going there again when we play Liverpool in the Premier League in 2020.

From the pie shop we walk about 100 yards to Klopp's Boot Room bar. What a stunning place. I am going to say now, this place could never exist in someone's imagination. It must have happened by mistake, or maybe it has just evolved. No-one could possibly have planned it. It is surreal. The entrance hall floor is artificial grass. As you go down the narrow stairs you walk under a 'This is Anfield' sign. And then, as you enter the fairly small area that is actually the boot room, you walk past a life-size cutout of Kloppy on your right, and on your left is a huge telly playing endless highlights of Liverpool's best goals. There is a tiny bar selling only bottled beers (choice of two brands) and the only soft drink available is Diet Coke. Next door, in the same house, and presumably owned by the same proprietor, is Klopp's B&B. In an article in the *Liverpool Echo*, to celebrate the opening of the establishment in August 2016, it proudly states that it plans to offer 10 beds.

From the Boot Room we walk about another 100 yards to The Flat Iron pub. Wow, this is another stunning place. A wedge-shaped building with beautiful windows looking out across the glorious old streets of Anfield. It is rammed with Liverpool supporters, but we get lucky and easily find a table with enough seats for all of us to sit down and enjoy a drink.

I will forever love this pub, not just because it is a beautiful building, with great staff and a friendly clientele, but most of all because when the Liverpool fans see Josh they instantly start to chant:

Only one John Bishop,
There's only one John Bishop,
There's only one John Bishop...

...quickly followed by:

Only one Jimmy Tarbuck,
There's only one Jimmy Tarbuck,
There's only one Jimmy Tarbuck...
Football supporters at their very best.

In the first half Liverpool had 82 per cent of the possession. Basically, we just couldn't get the ball. I have read a few silly comments about how defensive we were. For God's sake, how are you supposed to attack without the ball? We got to half time and somehow it was still 0-0. Things went better in the second half. We managed to get the ball a few times. We put together some good moves, and Loris Karius had to save a free kick from Graham Carey.

It was a truly awesome performance from Argyle. About 15 minutes from the end we started to talk about the replay. And then the countdown began. I have to admit that I had slightly stopped worrying about the Liverpool attacks by this time. It really did seem that they had run out of ideas about how to score against us. It was one of those situations, possibly the most extreme I have ever seen, where one team is pinned back around the penalty area and the other team is passing the ball around looking for a way through that just isn't there.

I do think this is a problem that the modern game has yet to address. How do you break down a massed defence? I was surprised that Liverpool didn't take a few more shots from outside the area. Surely it would be worth it? There is always the chance that one would find its way through, and also, if you don't score at least you have the chaos of the rebounds to work with too.

And here is the other thing I would have done: I would have scaled back on the high pressing and let Argyle have the ball a bit more to encourage us to come out of extreme defence. I mean to say, Liverpool were so superior in quality that withstanding a few attacks from Argyle shouldn't have been too much of a problem, and in return Liverpool would have got some space to play in. Fair dos, if you are playing Chelsea or someone else really good you don't want them to have the ball too much anywhere on the field, but Argyle? I reckon it would have been beneficial to allow us to lose our defensive attitude a bit more.

Buy hey, that didn't happen and the six minutes of added time came and went, and — can you believe it? — we drew 0-0 with Liverpool at Anfield. Possibly the greatest 96 minutes watching football that I have ever had.

I know there are people who can't stand Liverpool FC, in the same way that some people can't stand Manchester United, but at the risk of alienating some of my readers I am going to say that visiting Liverpool and Anfield was, for me, everything I ever imagined it would be, and more. To stand in that ground with 8,500 Argyle fans and listen to the Kop singing, 'You'll Never Walk Alone' was truly a great moment, and one I will never forget.

Our train from Liverpool pulls into Exeter station at 22.45 as scheduled, and there in the car park, safe and sound, is our trusty old Rav4. We climb in and set off up the long and winding road to Moretonhampstead. I've driven this road so many times. It has a tendency to go on and on and on, but tonight we are still buzzing from the great day we have just experienced. As I've said, Sarah gave up watching Argyle years ago, she couldn't stand the tension, nor cope with the disappointments, but tonight she is full of it. "When is the replay?", "Got to get a babysitter!", "Seriously, could Argyle maybe even beat Liverpool at Home Park?"

It seems like no time at all before we are pulling into our yard and our adventure is over.

"I'll tell you what, Sarah," I say, "you go in and put the kettle on, I've just got to check this one thing in the shed." As I walk over towards the door, I feel the wind and the Dartmoor drizzle on my face. I love this place so much. I open the door, flick on the light switch and glance towards the big red vice. Oh my God, the ticket has gone.

18TH JANUARY 2017, LIVERPOOL (H)

Now we have the small matter of the replay at Home Park. In the fourth-round draw last night, of course we were all hoping for Man U away. As it turned out, we drew Wolves at home. If we win against Liverpool at Home Park, beating Wolves at home will seem like a formality. I'm beginning to wonder if this book will ever end.

When we arrive at Home Park for the replay I have a strong feeling that, for the Argyle supporters, this is going to be a once-in-a-lifetime opportunity. The place is absolutely buzzing. I take the opportunity to buy a half-and-half scarf, which I have been thinking I might need for the cover of the book. I bought one at Anfield, but it was a little bit odd in that it was actually more of a sixty-forty scarf. The Argyle end looks like a bit of an add-on. The new one is bang on fifty-fifty, but it is missing the badges of both clubs. I'm hoping we can do some cutting and pasting to make up the perfect scarf.

I am standing around with Alex waiting for the turnstiles to open— that's two games in two weeks for him and he seems pretty relaxed. We are having a good laugh about the fact that he is going to be a lone Liverpool supporter sitting amongst thousands of Argyle fans. Suddenly the stewards begin to clear a way through to the main gates and then the Liverpool coach slowly makes its way into the ground. I double

check that I am actually awake and not dreaming —
the Liverpool coach arriving at Home Park! Even now,
hours later, I am filling up with emotion at the memory
of that moment. Come on, Derek Adams, please, please
get us into the Premier League. Come on, you can do it!

We lost the replay 1-0 but I am not kidding when I say I have never,
ever seen Argyle play as well as they played that night. Liverpool
had us on the ropes for the first 18 minutes, ending up with them
scoring from a corner. At one goal down our fear melted away, and
from that moment on we matched them until the final whistle. We
were superb! Will we see football as good as that at Home Park ever
again? Honestly, if you had come to that match not knowing who
the two teams were, you would have thought you were watching
a good game in the Premier League. OK, possibly I am straying
just a bit over the top there, but I don't care what anyone says, it's
a fact; we were just awesome.

These last couple of weeks have been the most fun I've
ever had as a football fan. Now we just have to stick
with it for the rest of the season and take that first big
step towards the Premier League. Next stop Stevenage
at home. Come on you Greens!

PART FOUR

THE STORY THAT NEVER ENDS

17TH APRIL 2017, NEWPORT COUNTY (H)

Three games from the end of the season and we have clinched promotion by beating Newport 6-1 at home in front of a 13,000 full house. It was a special day to be an Argyle fan for sure, but for me it was a great relief for another reason too. For months now I have had the feeling that, probably quite rightly, we have been playing with a bit more caution, and in the words of the football pundit, we have been doing what we have to do to get promoted. Some time well before Christmas the pretty football had dried up and a much more steely approach had been instilled in the team. Not so good to watch but the results, or more importantly the position in the League, have justified the change.

We were 2-0 up at half time and things were looking good, but as all football fans know 2-0 is 2-0, it's not three points and it's a scoreline that will always be tense until about two minutes from the end. Seven minutes into the second half Graham Carey made it three and then at last everyone could relax, including the players (and maybe even the manager, although he never looked that calm in truth) and for the rest of the game we were back watching the football that we all love to see. We were unstoppable. Three more goals (and yes, one for Newport) and then it was party time. We are back in League One, the third tier of English football, after seven seasons in League Two.

I'm driving back across the moor and the phone rings. That always really annoys me, because I worry that it might be something important that I need to attend to before I get home. After a few miles I decide that I can't go on without checking who it was, so I pull into a small car park overlooking the moor between Yelverton and Princetown. I check the phone and it was David, from Ockley Books. I decide to ring him back. Three rings and he picks up the phone.

"Hello."

"Hi, David, it's Tom here, how's it going?"

"Yeah, oh, hi, Tom." Then there is a delay. David always speaks really carefully, and he clearly thinks a lot about what he is about to say. Sometimes there are quite long hesitations while he works out which words to use. I always wonder if he's rung me up by mistake and doesn't actually have anything to say to me at all. And then, because the space is there, I start to speak myself.

"I'm just on my way back from the match, David, great result and great game to watch too."

"Yes, Tom, that's why I rang. I think, you know, what with you getting promoted and all, you can't really end the book where you have, you'll have to take it through to the end of the season."

"Ooh, I don't know about that, David, the thing is the story has ended. It was supposed to be a book about one game against Barnet, and it's gone on far beyond that already. It can't just keep going on and on."

"Well, I think, you know, last season's play-offs, then the games against Liverpool, and now promotion. You have to keep going, I mean it's even possible that you might still end up as champions."

"Yeah, that's crossed my mind too, but the trouble

is, David, I'm on to my next book now. I've left all that Alex stuff behind."

I was lying now, but I have been worrying about the book and whether it would be published in time for the new season, and I didn't want to delay it even more.

"Well, Tom, you have a think about it over the next day or two. I'll ring you on Tuesday. You can leave Alex out of it, but really, you do have to take it to the end of the season."

"OK, David, I'll think about it, but you know, we've signed the contract, and I have sent you the manuscript. I feel like I've finished with it and I just want to move on."

"Tom, just think about it. You know it makes sense, OK?"

"Yeah OK, David, I will."

"And by the way, congratulations on your promotion. And let's speak soon."

"OK, David, bye for now."

Wow, it's late on a Saturday afternoon and I've just had a phone call from David. He's obviously been thinking about the book more than I imagined. I decide to take a little wander on the moor to try to clear my head a bit, and to come to terms with having to write another section to the book.

I know David is right. It has been a phenomenal couple of seasons for Argyle, and it doesn't make any sense to miss out on what might be a very successful ending to the story. When I first had the idea for the book, or to be more accurate, when I first thought of the title, the idea was to write about the three days around the one game of Barnet away. I wanted to write about what it is like being an ordinary fan going to an ordinary match. I wanted to explore the experience of a human being who has associated himself with a football club, for no real reason other than that he lives reasonably nearby. I soon realised that my idea was going to require more literary skill than I actually have. But then, luckily for me, the book took on a life of its own as Plymouth Argyle fortuitously went on an 18-month run of success, now ending with promotion to League One.

***

I wander over to the old railway line that runs from Yelverton to Princetown. The line was opened in 1883 and was primarily used to transport granite from the quarries, and prisoners to Dartmoor Prison, which is situated in Princetown, right in the middle of the moor. In the 1930s when the roads became a more convenient form of transportation, business slowly decreased and the line was finally closed in 1956. I eventually reach the little bridge that some years ago featured in a television programme that simulated a break-out from the jail. The two pretend convicts rested awhile under the bridge before making their way off the moor towards Yelverton. I always think that if I ever had to escape from the jail I would head north. Agreed, it is the most inhospitable route off the moor, but it is also the route the guards would least expect you to take.

It is starting to get a little chilly so I wander back to the car and set off homewards. The radio is on but it is about the Exeter Chiefs who I have no interest in, so I turn down the volume. I am thinking about the title of the book, *Barnet Away*. It was just a text from Josh, and now it is almost a book. I find myself thinking about Robert Pirsig, and *Zen and the Art of Motorcycle Maintenance*. That's got to be the greatest title for a book ever. I wonder if he thought of the title before he thought of the book. As much as I loved the idea of the book, I never managed to finish reading it myself. The rather highbrow philosophy was all a bit too much for me. I gave up on it two-thirds of the way through. I once read that Pirsig's book had been rejected by 100 publishers before it was finally accepted for publication in 1974. In those days self-publishing was almost impossible, so if the publishers didn't go for it then you ended up with a huge pile of typed A4 sheets in a dusty box under your desk, while you cracked on with your next idea. Pirsig's book sold five million copies in the first few years after publication, and I would say most of them were bought because of the title. Now then, let's think about that: *Barnet Away*, that's a good title don't you think, surely that's got to be worth a hundred or so sales on its own! Maybe that's what persuaded David to give it a go.

***

I've been thinking about the book quite a bit for the last couple of days and I have decided that David is clearly right, I do have to add another section. So on the Monday morning I give him a call.

"David, hi, it's Tom." There's a bit of a delay while he works out who I am and then he thinks about what to say.

"Oh, hi, Tom."

"David, is it a good time to call, have you got five minutes?"

"Yes, sure ,Tom, no problem."

"I'm going to take the book to the end of the season, David, that's the right thing to do, isn't it. But you do realise it's a bit of a double-edged sword, don't you?"

"How's that,Tom?"

"Well, the thing is, the chances are we're going to finish second. We might even know that before the last game, and then I am going to be writing about being losers, whereas if we stopped now we're winners, do you see what I mean?"

"Yes, I see that, but what an opportunity to miss if you go on to be the champions, Tom, that's the thing."

"Yes," I reply, "I can see that, but it's a hell of a risk isn't it? I mean, Doncaster have to lose two games out of the three. That's not very likely is it? And then we have to win seven points out of nine. For some reason I am confident we can do that. But you know, only a few games ago Doncaster looked unbeatable, what with Darren Ferguson and all that."

"Tom, just do it, right? If it doesn't work out that's football, mate, that's the Beautiful Game. The book tells the story."

"OK, David, I agree. I'll crack on and I'll be in touch."

I put the phone down and make a coffee. What an end to the season. The next three Saturdays are going to be the best ever if you enjoy edge-of-your-seat excitement, which I don't, and I do, and I don't. Do you remember those beautiful Leonard Cohen lyrics, "I want you, I don't want you…"? I just had to put that in, in case you thought that last sentence was an editing error. Ah well, that's the beautiful game. So true, so true.

***

22 APRIL 2017, COLCHESTER UNITED (A)

		P	GD	PTS
1	DONCASTER	44	34	85
2	PLYMOUTH	44	24	82
3	PORTSMOUTH	44	32	78
4	LUTON	44	21	68

(* marks row 2, Plymouth)

Saturday comes and we are playing Colchester away. My whole day is designed around me needing to be in the house at 2.30 to tune in to the game. I actually love listening to the commentary on the radio. I do have to have something else to do at the same time though, so I usually clean the kitchen or tidy up my desk. It has to be a task that doesn't take much of my attention otherwise I drift away from the game, which is really annoying. If you are not paying attention you hear the excitement and then you have to wait to hear which end of the field the action is at to work out if things are good or bad. Concentration is the key when it comes to listening to football on the radio. Putting the phone out of reach is a must. Looking at that screen and listening to the radio just don't go together.

Doncaster are playing Wycombe. Wycombe need the points to stay in contention for the play-offs, but so do Colchester. I've got to be honest, I'm not feeling positive about this going our way.

Wycombe take the lead in the ninth minute. That feels good, but Doncaster equalise a few minutes later. Meanwhile, we are in a war of attrition hanging on to a 0-0 draw at Colchester. In the 32nd minute Wycombe go ahead again and amazingly go on to win the game. We hang on for our point at Colchester and we're still in the title race. I'm beginning to get a bit excited now. Oh my God, we could still win this, this is ridiculous, what's happened to Doncaster, how come they are falling to bits like this? Being a football fan often feels like asking yourself an endless series of such questions over and over until the end of the season. Then it's more questions about next year. Oh my God, come on you Greens. Could this happen against all the odds, could our dreams come true? Come on Argyle!

When the situation with Argyle gets as intense as it is at the moment I turn to anything and everything to get my fix. I read all the *Plymouth Herald* articles about Argyle, no matter how daft some of them are, and I listen to the excellent weekly podcasts with the paper's sports writer Chris Errington. Now there's a bloke who has made a nice career out of being an Argyle fan. I've never met him but I like the way he always manages to take such a loyal and balanced view of everything Argyle. I wouldn't say I always 100 per cent agree with his stance, but it is so much more restful than listening to some of the football chat shows on national radio.

Why do so many pundits feel that an essential part of making a good chat show involves being as rude and obnoxious as possible about just about everything? What's wrong with these guys? And then they wonder why no-one is phoning in. Call me old-fashioned, but if I wanted to express my opinion I'd like to be able to do it in a civilised situation, without needing to be some kind of hard-skinned back-room lawyer with the skills to defend myself against the kind of shark attacks dished out by bullying football pundits on the radio. Bring back the jolly old Home Service, that's what I say.

29TH APRIL 2017, CREWE ALEXANDRA (H)

		P	GD	PTS
I	DONCASTER	44	34	85
2	PLYMOUTH	44	24	82
3	PORTSMOUTH	44	32	78
4	LUTON	44	21	68

So, two games to go. We need Doncaster to lose one game and we need to win both our remaining games. I'm trying to remember the last time that I was this involved in an end-of-season dogfight. The two seasons that spring to mind are when Arsenal nicked the title from Liverpool in the 1988/89 season with a last-minute goal scored by Michael Thomas. And then, of course, in the 2011/12 season when Manchester City took the title out of United's hands with the last-minute Sergio Aguero goal. Both unbelievable finishes, but no comparison to how it feels right now being a Plymouth Argyle supporter. This is as tense as it gets and it feels as if it has been going on forever.

Over the last seven days I must have looked at that League table 20 or more times. Today Argyle host Crewe Alexandra, who have nothing to play for except their pride. Doncaster are away at Exeter City, who are themselves still in with a strong chance of making the play-offs. We need Exeter to win, a draw won't do, and then of course we have to win, and that will put us top of the League. Come on Exeter, you can do this for Argyle, and anyway, you have to win to make it to the play-offs. And then, of course, you have to win the play-offs so that we can play you twice next season to claim our free six points.

Unbelievably, some weeks ago, when it looked as if we were still worrying about whether we would make the play-offs ourselves, my wife Sarah had asked me if I minded if she went to a plant sale on this particular Saturday. At the time I was fully aware of the implications of her request. It meant that I would be at home looking after our granddaughter instead of being at the match. I have to be honest, I would always say, 'yes' to any request like this from Sarah without hesitation. Most times it's me asking if she would be OK if I go to the football, so the odd day that I can't go is fine by me. And let's face it, and to be brutally mercenary about it, it's always handy to give a little bit back now and again. I mean, what if Exeter win this afternoon, and we win too, I'm definitely going to want to go to Grimsby next Saturday, aren't I? So this vitally important penultimate game of the season at Home Park this afternoon, just happens to be one that I will be listening to on the radio.

***

I tune in at about 2.30pm, or to be more precise, I log in, as I use the Plymouth Player HD app on my phone to listen to the game. Sometimes, if it is an away game I go out to the shed and tune in to Radio Devon on the radio. That's ideal for me because I can clean some tools at the same time as listening to the game. Being in the shed, cleaning tools, listening to the Argyle commentary, is a situation very close to my perfect scenario. The home games aren't usually on the radio, presumably because it is felt that it discourages people from going to the match, which it probably does. And of course, the radio commentary of the game is a product that is worth some money, and the app is a great way of selling it.

The Player HD app costs me £5 a month, £60 a year, and I must listen to maybe 30 games throughout the season. It's good value for me. I presume Argyle get a fair bit of that money for providing that service. Today, because Sarah isn't here, I can turn the volume up pretty high, so I put the whole thing through the big old beatbox that Josh gave me a few years ago. Now I am all ready and set up to go.

I've just re-read that paragraph and I've got to say I am a bit worried about it. Is it all a bit unnecessarily technical? On reflection I have decided not to delete it. It might be a bit boring for sure, but the thing is this, in 10 years' time, if someone reads this book, they will be amazed at how primitive the technology was back in 2017 when a 66-year-old man on Dartmoor wanted to listen to a game of football. Let's go back in time and look at a sort of similar situation in history. Let's think about when you read a few pages of *Pride and Prejudice* and are gobsmacked by the palaver involved when Darcy needs to get a message to Elizabeth. You know, he has to get his horse out of the stable, put a saddle on it, and then ride like the wind. He doesn't just bosh out a few words on his phone and press the send button. Also, while we're on the subject of all this technology, I think I need to clarify one more thing. For those of you who haven't made the decision to just skim over this tech section of the book, the reason that I can't just take the whole Player HD set-up out to the shed, which would of course be my dream scenario, is that we don't get a phone signal up here on the moor, our phones work by courtesy of WiFi Call, which presently has a range of approximately 20 yards from our router. There must surely be a way of extending that signal to the shed, but I haven't worked it out yet. Maybe that is a job I should look into ready for next season. But then surely it won't be long before we get 4G, and then of course, we will all be happy forever.

***

It's 3pm and the match begins. And, as if to order, Crewe score very early on, to be precise in the sixth minute. Unbelievable, and now anything can happen. We need to push forward to score a couple of goals and if they then score on the break the whole game can so easily slip through our fingers. It's not that we aren't the better team, we clearly are, although in this particular game at the moment we're not, it is just the way games go, if you go a goal down there is a lot of pressure and sometimes it's difficult to stay calm. I'm getting in a bit of a state already and we still have 80 minutes to go. This has happened to us so many times this season. We really do need to work on a way of cutting back on conceding these early goals. It's always such a nightmare.

Oh my God, Exeter have taken the lead at Doncaster. We have to win, a draw won't do. This is madness. Surely it couldn't be that Exeter win and then we lose against Crewe. That would just be unbearable. Come on Argyle. I know we have ages to go yet, but Crewe are playing out of their skins.

Exeter's lead lasts exactly 10 minutes, but in a funny sort of way that has taken the pressure off. I'm slipping back into the less stressful state of not too much hope now. I smile as I listen to Chris Errington explaining that we have already won this season anyway by getting promoted. I know, I know, you're right, Chris, but you know it doesn't work like that. For a minute there we had a chance of being the champions, and now it's slipping away.

We get through to half time with no more goals in either game. Crewe are the better team but that doesn't really worry me. I've watched so many games where the better team loses. It's all about the goals, and you can be the better team for 85 minutes and in a few seconds you can concede a goal and lose the match. That's how football is. Over a period of time the better teams rise to the top for sure, but in a single game anything can happen.

The second half starts and Crewe are still playing really well. But I have a good feeling. There's nearly always a time in every game when a team has their purple patch, and we haven't had ours yet. And then the news comes through that Exeter have taken the lead again. Now, if things stay as they are we will go into the last game of the season with us needing to win, and Doncaster needing to lose, for us to be champions. But there is still half an hour to go, so much can change in half an hour. Meanwhile, Portsmouth have taken the lead at Mansfield. If Argyle and Doncaster both lose then Portsmouth will be well and truly back in the race.

We are now 70 minutes into the game and at last things are beginning to change. Derek Adams has brought on Nathan Blissett to play up front alongside Ryan Taylor. Suddenly it feels as if the players have realised what has got to happen here. Crewe are starting to look a bit rattled. And then it happens. Argyle get the equaliser from a corner when Taylor smashes in the loose ball. This feels a bit better now.

Five minutes later, in the 79th minute, Blissett gives us the lead with a brilliant header from another corner. And yes, in that moment we are top of the League. Come on you Greens.

Then we get the news that we really needed to hear. In the 86th minute Exeter go 3-1 up against Doncaster. For us, the most important part of that result is that Doncaster have lost, but for the Exeter fans, the most important thing is that they have definitely qualified for the play-offs. If we can hang on to our lead we will go into the last game of the season needing a win to end up as the champions of League Two. The minutes tick away. We survive a couple of scares, and then the final whistle blows. Everything, absolutely everything has gone our way. Being a fan of Plymouth Argyle doesn't get much better than this.

And now, everything comes down to Grimsby away. The top three teams go into the final game of the season with a chance of winning the League, but crucially for Argyle, the outcome is in our hands. A win next Saturday at Blundell Park and we are guaranteed to be the champions.

**

6TH MAY 2017, GRIMSBY TOWN (A)

			P	GD	PTS
*	1	PLYMOUTH	45	25	86
	2	DONCASTER	45	31	85
	3	PORTSMOUTH	45	34	84
	4	LUTON TOWN	45	25	74

I'm on my way to Grimsby to watch the final game of the season. The 5.30pm kick off means that the journey should be quite relaxed. As I pay for my parking ticket, I think back to the beginning of the book when I had all that drama en route to Barnet. The train pulls into the station and I look up at the clock and think about Einstein and the theory of relativity. It's not something I think about a lot actually, mainly because I simply don't understand a word of it. The theory of relativity is the point in the human understanding of existence where I get well and truly left behind. I'm fine until then. Evolution, atoms, molecules, reproduction, death and decay, and so on and so on, I get all that. But relativity, or should I say, the theory of it, is a step too far for me.

It is interesting though, because although I don't understand the theory of relativity in a physics kind of way, when it comes to looking at things from a more metaphysical perspective I find it easy to see that time and space are not constant. For instance, how do you measure space? That's always interested me. When the teacher said to me how long is a yard, and I correctly replied three feet, I always wondered but never said, "That's all very well mate, but how long is a foot?" The point being, what are you measuring it all against? A foot could be huge or it could be tiny, no-one really knows do they? In truth, the world might be tiny or it might be huge. It might all fit in a matchbox, or it might be absolutely enormous, or on the other hand it might be exactly the size that you imagine it to be. Who knows?

And if you are thinking, "oh dear, let's get back to the football", before we do let's just think about time for a minute. If you measure time with a clock, then yes a minute is exactly a minute and so on, but if you measure it by how long it is until the school bell goes, well, in French lessons it's ages, but in woodwork lessons it comes around all too quickly. And if you think about being a football supporter, when time is running out and your team needs to score a goal then time goes really quickly, but if you are hanging in there and your team is trying to prevent a goal being scored before the final whistle, then time really does seem to drag. Time is very definitely relative to what is happening then and there.

So there we are. Definitely not Einstein's theory of relativity, but definitely the real experience of being a human being. Time and space are not constant.

***

Sing when you're fishing!
You only sing when you're fishing!
Sinnnnng when you're fishing!
You only sing when you're fishing!

The mood amongst the Argyle fans inside Blundell Park is amazing. We are in the Osmond Stand at the east end of the ground. Built in 1939, I can officially state that it is the oldest football stand I have ever been in. Five feet in front of my seat is a vertical, 12-inch wide, riveted steel girder that actually prevents me from seeing either goal. I don't know whether to laugh or cry. As it turns out, before the kick off I am able to move two seats to my left and from there I get a perfect view. Wikipedia informs me that the Osmond Stand has a capacity of 2,000, of which 1,000 have a restricted view. On the same page I find out that Blundell Park is the lowest ground in England, built at two feet above sea level.

***

The game doesn't go our way. We concede an early goal after 42 seconds, and although we manage to equalise early in the second half, we simply can't find a way to score that all-important winning goal. We finish second in the league on goal difference.

GRIMSBY TOWN	1	1	**PLYMOUTH**
HARTLEPOOL	2	1	**DONCASTER**
PORTSMOUTH	6	1	**CHELTENHAM**

		P	W	L	D	GF	GA	GD	PTS
1	PORTSMOUTH	46	26	9	11	79	40	39	87
2	PLYMOUTH	46	26	9	11	71	46	25	87
3	DONCASTER	46	25	10	11	85	55	30	85
4	LUTON TOWN	46	20	17	9	70	43	27	77
5	EXETER CITY	46	21	8	17	75	56	19	71
6	CARLISLE	46	18	17	11	69	68	1	71
7	BLACKPOOL	46	18	16	12	69	46	23	70

***

One Derek Adams!
There's only one Derek Adams!
One Derek Ahhh-dams!
There's only one Derek Ahhh-dams!!

After a brief moment we're straight on to the next song,
this one sung to the tune of 'Achey-Breaky Heart':

We have Carey
Graham Carey
I just don't think you understand
He is Derek Adams' man
He is better than Zidane
We have Graham Carey!

After an hour or so of a very noisy end-of-season
promotion party, the Argyle fans are finally making
their way out of Blundell Park. The mood is surprisingly
upbeat considering the result. We had to win, and we
didn't, we drew. Doncaster Rovers lost, and Portsmouth
won and are champions. It's not the result we all wanted,
but the Argyle fans en masse have decided that it doesn't
really matter. We have had an amazing year and we are
playing in League One next season. I decide to walk
from the ground back to my hotel. I ask a policeman
for directions and he seems surprised that I am even
considering the walk. The truth is I like being on my
own, and a long walk will give me a chance to think
about the events of the last few hours.

Obviously this is not the ending that I wanted for the book. I wanted it to be a record of a triumphant season that simply could not have gone any better. But I feel fine. Today, in that ground the team did all they could and things just didn't go our way. The fans were amazing. I never thought I would say this, but today I feel proud to be a supporter of Plymouth Argyle. I've been to some fantastic games of football. In the last 18 months I have watched play-off semi-finals, a play-off final, some great local derbies, and this season, the two FA Cup games against Liverpool. But right now there is no doubt in my mind, today's game against Grimsby is up there as one of the best I've ever been to. Not because of the football either – to be honest, we played predominantly route one throughout the whole game. And certainly not because of the result, obviously we needed to win and didn't. The reason it was such a great game was because of the tremendous effort that all the players made, and the tremendous support that all the fans gave to the team. It was an awesome occasion.

The walk back to the hotel takes me through the industrial area between Cleethorpes and Grimsby, and then out on to the main road that connects the two towns. Living out on the moor as I do, I don't get to see much of city life, and when I do I am often shocked by what I see. To be honest, I am not surprised that some of the people in this area feel like they have been forgotten by the politicians. It certainly does look that way. I spot some Argyle fans who have also decided to walk and I tag on to the group for company. I have to admit I was a little scared there, being on my own. As we approach Grimsby my companions take the route towards the docks and I veer left towards the town centre.

On my own again and not a soul to be seen anywhere. It's only 8.30pm and it feels like it could be the middle of the night. The place is deserted. As I pass a furniture shop, a man lurches out of one of the doorways and comes towards me. The poor guy looks as if he is a rough sleeper. He isn't that steady on his legs and I think to myself, "I'll take him on if I have to". And then I think, "what the hell am I thinking? I'm a 66-year-old man, not bloody Rambo". I hold on to my phone. Now we are close and we look into each other's eyes.

"Evening, mate," I say, to try to find out where he is at.

"Alright, pal?" he replies, as he lurches past me.

We both carry on our journeys. Phew, I can't wait to get back to my hotel room.

I reach the town centre and still not a soul anywhere. Failed businesses and boarded-up shops all around me. This is the marketplace that is the modern world. I don't like it much and it makes me feel sad. And then I remember why I love my garden, and why I spend so much time watching football. And I think of Alex, and my shed. And I think of going to watch Argyle with my sons. Football is an OK thing to be involved in, isn't it?

BY HENRY WIDDICOMBE

I doubt I'm alone in feeling like I've spent most of my life working on the relationship with my dad. Not specifically *my* dad — although there's possibly a good number who feel like it about him — what I mean is, I'm sure there are plenty of people who feel the same way about their dads. And I don't think it's any coincidence that the times I've felt that Dad and I are onto something is when our support of Argyle has been active rather than passive. This has fallen mainly into two periods: what I fondly recall as the glory years of the 1990s/early-2000s (Neil Warnock, Paul Sturrock, Ian Holloway; heady days), and right now as the club experiences a slow but utterly delightful recovery from the absolute brink of extinction, under James Brent and Derek Adams.

That's not because football is the extent of our relationship, in fact far from it. Football is the background noise. The reason there's no awkward re-establishment of the relationship each time we meet. The life raft we cling to that allows us to dive into any topic we care to take on, because we've always got Argyle. Whatever conversational backwater we sail down, the good ship Mayflower is always within sight. Speculating about exactly how good a manager Derek Adams is, or how long we can expect to hold on to him. Discussing whether you can actually play your way out of the lower Leagues, or whether brute strength is the best, but ultimately dullest, route to progression. Wondering what we think the pasties will be like at the away ground we're visiting for the first time. All great topics to get you out of a conversational jam. And, conversely, I reckon there are games I've been to with Dad where the most we've done is exchange a hug and the most basic pleasantries, and yet the shared experience of doing something we both love is enough to bring us closer together.

I know Dad likes us to win, and I'm certain Josh hates losing. Me, I'm more in it for the experience. I love being an underdog, and I genuinely don't mind the feeling of losing; I kid myself that it builds character. Of course, I like us to win, but I know that I've experienced far more emotion as a lower League fan of my local team than the majority of my friends who just picked a team from the top flight at around the same age that I decided to be a Green. It also means that times like now when we're actually trying to play football — a pretty rare experience in the lower Leagues — become all the more special.

It was interesting to read that Dad said he knew that my favourite memory would be when we won the 50/50. Don't get me wrong, it's a classic memory (he actually made us share that money with our siblings, who hadn't been suffering on the terraces week in week out, and I never quite got over that betrayal), but my actual favourite Argyle memories are all linked to specific players. You see a lot of players come and go when you support a team that has no money and for large parts of my life have struggled even to assemble a squad in time for the start of the season. Sometimes a player washes up on your shores who's a little bit special, they're a class above the rest of the team, and you spend the whole time worrying about how long you can keep hold of them, or just how exactly they came to be plying their trade in Plymouth. One wet weekend, word will go round that there's a scout from Sheffield Wednesday in the grandstand, and sure enough within weeks the player is refusing to sign a new contract and off they pop on a Bosman in July. Many stand out for me: Akos Buszaky, Carlo Corrazin, getting Scott Sinclair in on loan. The types of player you get excited about every time the ball even bounces in their general direction.

My all-time favourite was Paul McGregor. A sulky, lazy, blond mod whom we got from Nottingham Forest, at a time when getting someone from Nottingham Forest still meant something. McGregor was incredibly frustrating in that 90 per cent of the time you felt like he knew full well he was better than the League he was playing in and couldn't give two craps about football anymore. I mean, he had been in Britpop band Merc, so who can blame him if his mind was elsewhere? And then 10 per cent of the time, he was possibly one of the most exciting players I've seen wear the green-and-white. Flashes of absolute footballing genius. One volley from outside the box I recall in particular. I've no idea if my memory is anything like what actually happened in real life, but thinking about it still gives me goosebumps. I can remember Josh and I pegging it down to the front of the Lyndhurst to celebrate, but again this could be a supplanted memory from any goal scored during that period. Anyway, during one of our recent life-raft moments I brought up the majestic Paul McGregor in conversation and it turned out Dad had absolutely no recollection of him. I could hardly believe my ears. No memory of Plymouth Argyle's player of the season 1999-2000! It just goes to show that while we think we're sharing exactly the same thoughts and emotions during a game, we're all actually picking our own moments that excite and stay with us.

Josh, my dad and I have this dream that in around 20 years when we're all retired (that's the first unlikely part), we'll go to all of Argyle's away games. Once a fortnight meeting up in a new town or city, another British backwater on a rainy Tuesday or, my favourite, on a balmy September Saturday waiting for the sun to descend over another dreadfully named stand so you can actually see the action for the glare. Dad still packing the flask of tea, and all three of us continuing to take a punt on the 50/50 knowing we'll not even hear the numbers through the inferior tannoy system installed in the away end. It sure sounds like heaven to me.

SO NOW THIS TALE IS FINISHED A FEW ASSORTED ENDNOTES AND FACTS THAT YOU MIGHT BE INTERESTED IN IF YOU'VE STAYED WITH ME THIS LONG:

* * *

In 2015, the former Padbury United chairman, 69-year-old Dr Phil Smith, was awarded a MBE for services to business and the community. Dr Smith is currently helping run Stoney Stratford FC.

* * *

In the 2015/16 season Padbury United, now renamed Padbury Village, finished third in the third tier of the North Bucks and District League.

* * *

In the 2015/16 season John Akinde played 47 games for Barnet. He was the third highest goal scorer in League Two with 23 goals, plus he made eight assists. Barnet finished the season in 15th position.

* * *

Jim McIntyre led Ross County to their first major trophy, the Scottish League Cup, beating Hibernian 2-1 in the final in March 2016.

* * *

The Mayflower Stand is currently scheduled to be redeveloped by the end of the 2018/19 season. The plan is to modernise the existing stand and keep the 'art deco façade' (turnstiles), with the aim of retaining the unique character of Home Park. Hats off to the chairman, he is in tune with at least one other Argyle fan on that one.

***

Martin Allen requested to leave Barnet on 1st December 2016. He took over as manager at Eastleigh FC playing in the Vanarama League. He was relieved of his duties 12 weeks later after having taken 11 points from his 15 games in charge.

***

Rossi Eames, the Barnet youth team coach, became the caretaker first team manager at Barnet on 1st December 2016. He took 17 points from the 12 games that he was in charge. Eames was replaced as manager on 15th February by ex-Argyle striker Kevin Nugent. After picking up only seven points from 11 games, Nugent was released on 15th April. Eames was again appointed as caretaker manager and picked up two more wins from the last four games of the season. He was given the role of head coach of Barnet FC on a permanent basis on 19th May 2017.

***

Lucky Spinner officially entered the 2016/17 Super 6 competition in August 2016 and joined our League. Gary Guesstimate entered the competition in Round 15. Our league ended the 2016/17 season with seven members.

LANGDON LEAGUE FINAL STANDINGS 2016/17

		PTS
1	JOSH	389
2	TOM	386
3	TONY	374
4	HENRY	372
5	ALEX	309
6	GARY GUESSTIMATE	287
7	LUCKY SPINNER	253

* * *

END OF SEASON SUPER 6 LEADERBOARD STATS

	OVERALL POSITION	PTS	AVG PER ROUND
ERIC RICHARDSON	1ST	501	10.02
IAN CHAPMAN	2ND	496	9.92
JOSH	106,065TH	389	7.78
TOM	172,632ND	386	7.72
LUCKY SPINNER	855,833RD	253	5.06

* * *

In the 36 rounds that Gary Guesstimate played Super 6 this season he averaged 7.97 points.

* * *

In the 2016/17 season Plymouth Argyle went behind to an early goal in seven of their 46 league games.

* * *

Liverpool clinched their place in the Champions League
on the last day of the season with a 3-0 win over
Middlesborough. I watched the whole game on Sky and
I don't remember seeing them play one long ball.

* * *

Exeter City reached the League Two play-off final
and lost 2-1 to Blackpool at Wembley. Alex was
there among the Exeter fans.

* * *

Paul Cook left Portsmouth to become the new manager at
Wigan Athletic on 31st May 2017. Seven months after leaving
Rotherham, Kenny Jacket became the new manager
of Portsmouth on 2nd June 2017.

* * *

Robert Pirsig died on 24th April 2017, aged 89. His second
book, *Lila,* was published in 1991, 17 years after *Zen and the
Art of Motorcycle Maintenance*. Prior to his death, both these
books were available secondhand on Amazon for 1p plus £2.80
postage. They are currently available for £3.22 each, plus
£2.80 postage.

* * *

In a moment of supreme weakness I sold the swan shot
gang mould for £30. I have regretted it ever since.